THE WIND BOOK
FOR RIFLE SHOOTERS

If you don't like what the wind is doing, just wait a minute—it will change.

THE WIND BOOK FOR RIFLE SHOOTERS

HOW TO IMPROVE YOUR ACCURACY IN MILD TO BLUSTERY CONDITIONS

LINDA K. MILLER AND CAPT. KEITH A. CUNNINGHAM (RET.)

Skyhorse Publishing

This is the first-ever guide to wind reading for target shooters. It is dedicated to the world-class wind-reading experts who generously shared their wisdom with us, and to the newcomers to our sport, who will benefit from their generosity.

———————————————————

Skyhorse Publishing books may be purchased in bulk at special discounts for sales promotion, corporate gifts, fund-raising, or educational purposes. Special editions can also be created to specifications. For details, contact the Special Sales Department, Skyhorse Publishing, 307 West 36th Street, 11th Floor, New York, NY 10018 or info@skyhorsepublishing.com.

Skyhorse® and Skyhorse Publishing® are registered trademarks of Skyhorse Publishing, Inc.®, a Delaware corporation.

Visit our website at www.skyhorsepublishing.com.

10 9 8 7 6 5 4

Library of Congress Cataloging-in-Publication Data is available on file.

Cover design by Brian Peterson
Cover photo credit: Linda Miller

Print ISBN: 978-1-5107-3972-7
Ebook ISBN: 978-1-5107-3974-1

Printed in China

TABLE OF CONTENTS

TABLE OF FIGURES

PREFACE AND ACKNOWLEDGMENTS

We sat down at the computer intending to write a very simple story, a story that would explain the simple thought process that we use to read the wind. (This became chapter 2.) Then we thought about some of the techniques and tactics that we use to win matches, and decided that the story wouldn't be complete without them (chapter 3). Since we believe that all these things are learnable, we then wrote about the underlying skills that support the process and the techniques (chapter 4). By then, the story was too long for anything but this book, so we added some of the things we wish we had known before we started—the basics (chapter 1) and words of wisdom from masters all over the world (chapter 5). Finally, we just had to have a conclusion.

Here it is . . . everything we wish we'd known before we started, instead of our having to learn as we went along, in concise, easy-to-read terms, with no mathematical bafflegab (well, not very much of that). Just straightforward guidance on what to do and especially on *what to think*.

The Wind Book for Rifle Shooters represents the first time shooters from all over the world have contributed to a book on shooting. The first edition included both our "kitchen-table" version and the Paladin-Press version. Both were published with our heartfelt thanks to everyone who made it possible:

Rick Ashton

Serge Bissonnette

Bert Bowden

Don Brook

Jim Bullock

George Chase

Stuart Collings

Keith Cunningham

Clint Dahlstrom

Darren Enslin

Stan Frost

Alain Marion

Arnold Parks

Jim Paton

Sandy Peden

Ed Pocock III

Bill Richards

John Simpson

Pat Vamplew

Mike Wong Shui

Charles F. Young

And the many authors who went before us all

The second edition is published with special thanks to our readers who provided suggestions (such as adding information on reading the wind in Olympic-style 50-meter ranges) and to "The King of 2 Miles" Eduardo Abril de Fontcuberta, who provided Words of Wisdom on extreme long-range wind reading.

INTRODUCTION

All other things being equal, it is a shooter's ability to read the wind that will make the most difference in the score. Once the shooter has acquired the best possible equipment, learned to fire a perfect shot, and learned to center the group, there is only one technical skill left to master. When you look at the winners and those who almost win, it will often be those who best handle the wind who finally finish at the top. However, the converse is not true; reading the wind is no substitute for being able to fire consistently perfect shots. The wind-reading experts whom we researched for this booklet were quick to emphasize this point. As George Stidworthy observed many years ago in *Rifle* magazine, while top shooters lose more points to wind than for any other reason, wind reading is less than half the story—the shooter's ability to group well provides the most important information he needs in order to read the wind. As Des Burke wrote, "a chronically poor holder has little chance of becoming skillful at wind judging. It brings to mind the old adage that the best holder is the best wind judge."[1]

The importance of a good hold cannot be overstated. Those target rifle shooters who have switched to F-Class (where their hold is improved by the use of a bipod or rest) see their scores jump up immediately. As one top-notch target rifle shooter put it, "It's amazing how much better their wind reading becomes when their hold improves!"

Of all the things that you can prepare, train, and plan for, reading the wind is probably the most difficult. It is the component of the match that is the most variable—changing by the minute. Following the marksmanship principles to ensure you fire a perfect shot will never change from range to range or day to day. But the wind is always changing, and the correct indicators to watch will vary from moment to moment. You cannot plan ahead for this; you must think on your hind legs, understand the peculiarities of the specific range, decide on the best wind-reading techniques to use, and then apply them to the situation. As David Tubb observed in *Highpower Rifle*, top shooters are probably excellent wind readers, but "what matters is what you do about what you read."[2]

We have frequently approached the "big guys," the men and women who consistently shoot good scores through all kinds of wind conditions, and asked, "So, what do you think about the wind?" Most would take a quick glance downrange and say, "Start with 8 minutes."[3] They often can't explain what they do to read the wind—they just know that they do it, and they get results.

We have been left thinking, "Great advice, coach . . . but how do you know? How do you figure it out? How do you do it? What are the questions you need to answer to be right so often? What is your thought process? How do you *think* about reading the wind?"

In trying to answer our own questions, we came to three important conclusions:

1. There is an overall procedure and a specific thought process for each wind decision. All shooters use one (or several), whether consciously or not. Experts are largely unaware of their own thought processes and conse-quently cannot articulate them well, though they use them very successfully. This is the focus of chapter 2.
2. There are techniques and tactics that are applied according to the situation, and these can be identified and learned, and collected in your wind-reading toolbox. This is the subject of chapter 3.
3. There are underlying skills that can be practiced and improved, developing your ability to read the wind consistently more accurately. These are covered in chapter 4.

Another thing we noticed during our research was that most top wind readers know their facts. They may not fully understand the high-level mathematics behind the facts, but they understand completely the application of the facts to the art of wind reading. We also noticed that many lesser shooters do not understand the facts or are unaware of them, or know only some of the facts and do not have a complete picture. We have assembled information from many sources into an easy-to-read summary of important facts in chapter 1.

Finally, in discussing wind reading with many world-class shooters, we realized that we weren't the only ones who wanted to know how they think about the wind, so we have included their thoughts and guidance in chapter 5. All these shooters generously shared their thoughts with us and gave us their kind permission to share them with you. We thank them for their wisdom and their generosity. If their words help you, please let them know when you see them on the range.

CHAPTER 1

WIND BASICS

"Technical data used to compute wind drift are ballistic coefficient, lag time, cross-range wind speed, and atmospheric conditions ... I love playing with computers, but in practical terms, most of what I know about bullet drift came from varmint shooting."[1] —Bill McRae

INTRODUCTION TO WIND BASICS

The aerodynamic efficiency of a bullet, its ability to overcome air resistance, is expressed as its ballistic coefficient. This shapes its trajectory. This also affects the bullet's ability to "buck the wind" or overcome the force of the wind. In addition, the higher the bullet's velocity, the flatter its trajectory. The flatter the bullet's trajectory, the less time it spends in the air. And the less time the bullet spends in the air, the less the wind deflection.

The bullet in flight is acted on by two forces: gravity and air resistance.[2] It is also affected by several factors, including altitude, humidity, temperature, barometric pressure, bullet drift, and wind.

Gravity acts on the bullet throughout its flight, gradually pulling it back to earth. Much like a baseball thrown to the batter, the bullet must be launched in a slightly upward direction in order to travel the distance required before falling back to earth. A bullet typically travels at about 1,400 miles per hour (about 2,000 mph at the muzzle, and more than 800 mph by the time it reaches a target 1,000 yards away).[3] The bullet's total flight time at 1,000 yards is about 2–3 seconds. Even at these speeds, the typical bullet used in target rifle matches requires about 40 minutes of elevation correction at 1,000 yards. Because of gravity, however, the bullet never reaches the lofty heights of the sight setting; in fact, the tables indicate that a Sierra 155-grain match bullet launched toward a target 1,000 yards away culminates at a height of 122 inches (about 10 feet).[4]

Air resistance (or drag) slows the bullet as it flies. The bullet starts to slow immediately upon leaving the muzzle. The bullet slows more and more as it flies; therefore, as noted in the FBI's *Advanced Rifle Training*, the bullet is slowing down throughout its flight, so that its average speed for the first half of a 1,000-yard shot will be much faster than its average speed for the second half. In fact, the average speed for each successive 100-yard segment of its flight is slower and takes longer.[5] The aerodynamic efficiency of the bullet determines just how much it will slow during that flight. For a given bullet, its initial velocity (or muzzle velocity) ultimately determines its total time in flight.

Altitude affects air resistance and therefore time in flight. The higher the altitude, the less air resistance, because the air is "thinner." Humidity also affects air resistance and therefore time in flight. Contrary to what common sense might indicate, the more humid the air, the less air resistance, because water vapor is actually lighter than air![6]

Air temperature and air pressure affect velocity—and trajectory. Under normal circumstances, this will affect your elevation only, and then only slightly. Under extreme circumstances (e.g., a bullet slowed by very cold temperatures, very high barometric pressures, fighting a very strong headwind), you may find that the bullet's sensitivity to wind increases enough to be noticeable.

During its flight, the rifle bullet is subject to "drift." Because the rifling in the barrel sets the bullet spinning, the bullet pulls itself in the direction of its spin. So, a bullet flying with a clockwise spin drifts to the right. This effect is largely unnoticeable at short range, but when we are shooting at 1,000 yards (900 meters) the effect is approximately 1 minute of angle (MOA).

Of all these factors, the most significant for lateral displacement of your bullet is the wind.

Wind is air in motion, and since air is the medium of transport for the bullet, that motion affects the path of the bullet in flight. So, the better you understand the behavior of the wind, the better you will understand the behavior of your bullet.

"The amount of deflection caused by the wind is determined by the direction of the wind, its velocity, and the range to the target. The greater the range, the longer the wind will have to move the bullet. And the faster the wind blows, the faster it will move the bullet. Wind deflection is not a constant curve. Just like the trajectory, the wind deflection curve is parabolic (i.e., constantly increasing). Therefore, the deflection at 400 yards will be more than twice the deflection at 200 yards."[7]

Wind is a vector force, having both direction and intensity. The amount of deflection that a given wind produces on your bullet is a factor of three things:

1. The velocity of the wind[8]
2. The direction of the wind
3. The distance the bullet travels or the time in flight

Estimating Wind Velocity

An estimation of wind velocity can be made by observation or by measurement.

Standard Terms	Mph	Kph	Ft/ sec	Description and Observations
	0-1	0-2	0-2	Calm. Smoke and dust rise vertically.
	1-3	2-5	2-4	Light air. Smoke and dust drift slowly. Barely felt.
Gentle	4	6	6	Slight breeze. Leaves rustle. Felt on face.
Moderate	8	13	12	Moderate breeze. Leaves & twigs in motion.
Fresh	12	19	18	Fresh breeze. Small branches move.
Strong	16	25	24	Strong breeze. Small trees sway.
Very strong	20	32	29	Very strong breeze. Large branches sway.

Figure 1. Wind velocity chart—natural objects.

Observation of Natural Objects

Figure 1 correlates the velocity of wind to natural things you can observe, such as smoke, dust, and vegetation. You can use these examples to get started in making your own observations and customizing your own chart.

While flags are the standard that competition shooters use to assess the wind velocity, it can be handy to have a description of the behavior of natural objects (e.g., grass, leaves, branches) at various wind velocities. This can be helpful when you are faced with a new range with flags of unknown material or when you are assigned a firing point where you can see the trees better than the flags.

Some ranges will not have sufficient natural material to provide you with the relevant observations. For example, at De Wet Range in Bloemfontein, South Africa, there is very little in the way of long grass or trees to use for this; however, you soon start using the angle of blowing sand as an indicator of wind speed (and direction). At Connaught Ranges in Ottawa, Canada, only the extreme right and left sides of the ranges provide clearly visible trees, although there is grass everywhere. At a World Cup match in Cuba, we found that a low-growing cover plant in front of the smallbore line was a better wind indicator than the flags. At Stickledown Range in Bisley, England, the best wind indicator (when it is present) is mirage on the edge of the gully about 600 yards uprange from the targets.

Wind Meters

Using a handheld wind meter or weather station is a good way to train your observation skills and to familiarize yourself with the conditions before you start the match. (Most match rules ban the use of such meters during firing.)

When you visit a range that is new to you, you can use a wind meter to acclimatize yourself to the natural wind indicators that are present. A wind meter can be a valuable training aid, especially when a shooter is calibrating the flags on the range. While there is a "standard" flag (specifying the weight of the fabric and the dimensions of the flag) in the Bisley "Bible," other ranges commonly have very different flags.

You can also use the wind meter to train your judgment when you're trying to learn to estimate the wind velocity by feel. Whenever you feel the wind on your face, stop and think about the feeling, and then take a wind meter reading. Associate that reading with the feeling. As you develop the skill, start to estimate the wind before you take the reading. Gradually your estimates will become more and more accurate.

The primary disadvantage of the wind meter is that it samples and measures only the wind at its location, whereas the bullet must fly hundreds of yards, possibly through many different wind conditions.

Flags

Most ranges that are intended for target rifle competition have wind flags. There are charts (an example follows) that describe the angle of "standard" (i.e., British) range flags at five wind velocities. The accuracy of this scale depends on the weight of the flags. (Dimensions, fabric, and humidity are the key factors in the effective weight of the flag.) "The use of heavier flags extends the upper limit of their usefulness for wind judging."[9]

In addition, the flag needs to be affixed to the pole by a halyard, so that it can pull away and fly higher than horizontal. The poles must be tall enough to show the shooter what the wind is doing at the height the bullet will fly (about 10 feet or more for a .308 at 1,000 yards).[10]

To read the flag diagrams, look at the height of the tip of the flag as it relates to the hoist of the flag. The dotted horizontal lines in Figure 2 will help you see the relationship between the fly end (tip) and hoist. Each horizontal line represents half the height of the hoist. For example, a "fresh" wind lifts the flag so that the tip of the flag is parallel with the base of the hoist, while a "strong" wind lifts the flag so that the tip of the flag is parallel with the middle of the hoist. Some range flags are made with two colors so that the centerline of the flag (running from the middle of the hoist to the tip) is more easily seen.

Most shooters at most ranges probably use the flags to estimate wind velocity. Shooters usually modify the scale to accommodate the specific range flags they are using. For example, you can use the British scale for Bisley flags, but you need to modify the scale for the shorter, lighter flags at Connaught Ranges in Canada. Figure 2 refers to standard target rifle flags (heavy flags, as used at ranges such as Bisley).

"At Bisley, the Stickledown Range flags are 15 feet long, 6 feet deep at the hoist, and about 12 inches deep at the fly.

For the shorter distances on the Century Range (300, 500, 600 yards), they are two-thirds this size."[11]

On the range, you will need to notice not only the angle that the flag is flying from the pole, but also some details of its behavior in the wind, such as:

- The number and speed of the ripples in the material
- The detailed behavior of the tip of the flag
- The "starch" of the flag, or how stiff it appears
- The sound of the flag at higher velocities

"As the wind reaches the higher values, one sees more changes in animation of the flag and less change in its height. The degree of animation, the noise of the flapping streamers, and, in some cases, the bending of the pole itself to the leeward may be the only clues to the great increase of wind speed."[12]

The following series of flag pictures are provided to give you an opportunity to study the details of a flag as the wind velocity changes.

For a quick, field-expedient approximation of the wind velocity, observe the angle of the flag as it lifts from the pole. Divide this angle by 4 or 5 (depending on the flag material) to get wind speed in miles per hour. For example, a flag flying at 90 degrees from the pole (straight out) indicates a wind speed of about 18–22 mph (90 divided by 5 is 18; and 90 divided by 4 is about 22).

Standard Terms	Mph	Kph	Ft/ sec	Description	Flag angle	Flag
	0-1	0-2	0-2	Flag hangs limply on the pole.		
	1-3	2-5	2-4	Flag moves to the lee side of the pole.		
Gentle	4	6	6	Flag lifts off the pole and flutters.	15°	
Moderate	8	13	12	Flag is definitely clear of the pole.	30°	
Fresh	12	19	18	Flag centerline is usually clearly visible.	60°	
Strong	16	25	24	Flag is straight out and getting "starched."	90°	
Very strong	20	32	29	Flag is flying above horizontal. The fewer the ripples, the faster the wind.	Above horizontal	

Figure 2. Wind velocity chart—flags

Figure 3. Flags showing gentle-to-moderate wind.

Figure 4. Flags showing fresh-to-strong wind.

Build Your Own Wind Chart

We suggest that you start with the most appropriate wind chart in the Tools Appendix and build your own charts to describe the conditions and flags for each range you shoot on. This will help you observe and assimilate your observations, and you will find it easier and easier to estimate the velocity of the wind.

Wind Direction

Probably the most neglected aspect of wind reading is fully understanding and correctly assessing the effects of wind direction. Because human beings sense wind velocity changes on their bodies more readily than wind direction changes, shooters often notice a velocity change, though they often miss a direction change. In many cases, wind direction

changes can have a greater effect on the bullet than wind velocity changes, as you will see later in this chapter (in the section on wind values).

Fundamentals of Wind Direction

The direction of the wind is always described in terms of its source; that is, the direction it is coming from. A "northwest wind" comes from the northwest.

A "left wind" comes from the left.

When shooters are describing the wind, the shooter is the "destination" of the wind, and the direction of the wind is described in terms of the source. A wind that moves from the targets to the shooter is a headwind. A wind that comes from behind the shooter is a tailwind. A left wind comes from the shooter's left. Wind from the left moves the bullet to the right.[13]

Like a rowboat crossing a river, the bullet is pushed sideways by the wind. If you attempt to cross the river exactly perpendicular to the current, you will have the greatest force of the water pushing on the side of your boat. By the time you have propelled the boat across the river, no matter how hard you try to go straight across, you will have been pushed downstream and will land some distance downstream on the opposite bank.

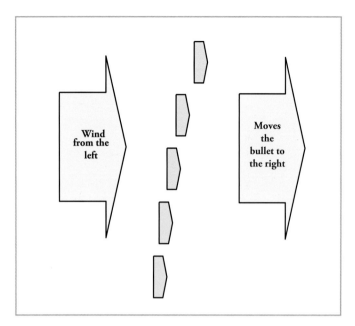

Figure 5. Wind acting on bullet.

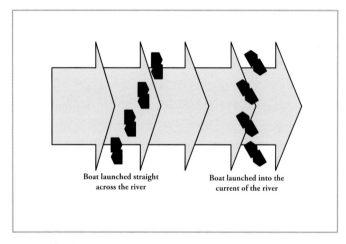

Figure 6. Boat crossing river.

If you want to land your boat on the opposite shore exactly across from your launch point, you must aim the boat upstream exactly the right amount so that the river current pushes you toward your target as you paddle forward. This is exactly what we do in rifle shooting: we launch the bullet into the wind to compensate for the amount it will blow us downwind toward our target while the bullet is in flight.

The Wind Clock

Many charts refer to the angle of the wind in terms of the hours of a clock. This is a common reference system used to describe wind direction.

Imagine the shooter, as he lies on the mound, as if he were at the center of a huge clock face, as shown in the wind clock diagram (Figure 7). The numbers on the inside of the circle represent the hour numbers on a clock. Headwinds are referred to as 12 o'clock winds, because they come from the 12 o'clock direction. Tailwinds are called 6 o'clock winds. Winds directly from the right are called 3 o'clock winds, and winds directly from the left are called 9 o'clock winds.

Many shooters also refer to wind direction in compass degrees. The numbers on the outside of the circle in the wind clock diagram represent degrees. Normally, shooters use only 0 degrees through 90 degrees, representing wind parallel to the shooter through to wind perpendicular to the shooter. They then repeat the same numbers for each quadrant, as shown in Figure 7. So the shooter may refer to a "90-degree wind from the left."

Wind "Values"

Wind from 90 degrees, a crosswind, produces the greatest deflection on the bullet. The amount of deflection of bullets (or boats) decreases as the angle of the wind (or the water) decreases; that is, wind from 60 degrees produces less deflection than wind from 90 degrees.

Wind that is parallel to the flight of the bullet (headwind or tailwind) produces negligible sideways deflection.[14] This means that the "value" or force of the wind varies according to the angle from which it is acting. Therefore, many shooters refer to the angle of the wind in terms of its value.

• A crosswind (a wind blowing from 90 degrees) is called a full-value wind, because it represents the maximum or full amount of deflection that can be caused by wind of a given velocity.

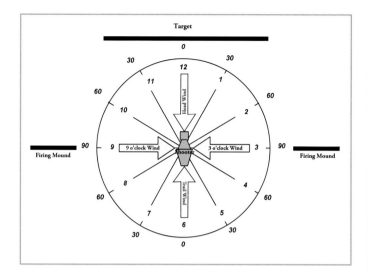

Figure 7. The wind clock.

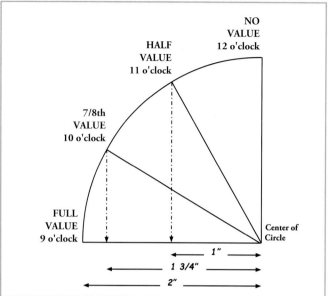

Figure 8. Wind values.

• A headwind or tailwind is called a zero-value or a no-value wind, because it does not deflect the bullet sideways at all.

• A half-value wind is a wind that produces half the force of a crosswind. The wind that delivers this amount of force blows from about 1 o'clock, 5 o'clock, 7 o'clock, or 11 o'clock.

Many people wrongly believe that a half-value wind blows from 45 degrees to the line of fire (halfway between 9 o'clock and 12 o'clock). Thus, there is considerable confusion around what a half-value wind really is. The following mathematical explanation should clarify the situation.

As mentioned earlier, wind is a vector force. Simply, that means it has both magnitude (speed) and direction. We can "resolve" or describe any vector in terms of its relative amounts of forward and sideways force. For example, in the wind values diagram (Figure 8):

• A vector from the 12 o'clock position to the center of the circle has zero lateral force, because it does not need

to move sideways at all to reach the center; it needs only to move forward.

• A vector from the 9 o'clock position to the center of the circle has all lateral force and no forward force, because it must move 2 inches sideways (and not at all forward) to reach the center.

• If we look at the amount of sideways movement that is required to travel from the 10 o'clock position to the center of the circle, we can see that it is just a little less than it took from the 9 o'clock position, about ⅞ of the distance.

• If we look at the amount of sideways movement that is required to travel from the 11 o'clock position to the center of the circle, we can see that it is half of the distance that it took from the 9 o'clock position. This is, in fact, the true "half-value" of wind. Some shooters memorize the full-value deflections for each range and then apply the ⅞ value for 10 o'clock, 2 o'clock, 8 o'clock, and 4 o'clock. And then they apply the half-value for 11 o'clock, 1 o'clock, 7 o'clock, and 5 o'clock.

For example, using the wind values applied chart below (Figure 9):

- If the full-value deflection of a 20 mph wind at 1,000 yards is 20 MOA, then its ⅞ value would be 17½ minutes, and its half value would be 10 minutes.

To refine these increments, some shooters would interpolate the intermediate values that are shown in the chart. A headwind or a tailwind would be zero value.

O'clock	Value	Examples in Minutes of Angle				
		300 y	500 y	600 y	900 y	1000 y
0900	Full value	3½	7½	10	18	20
0930		3½	7½	10	18	20
1000	⅞ value	3	6½	8¾	15¾	17½
1030	⅔ value	2¼	5	6½	12	13¼
1100	Half value	1¾	3¾	5	9	10
1130	¼ value	¾	1¾	2½	4½	5
1200	No value	0	0	0	0	0

Figure 9. Wind values applied.

O'clock	Deflection discount	Examples in Minutes of Angle				
		300 y	500 y	600 y	900 y	1000 y
0900	None	3½	7½	10	18	20
0930	Negligible	3½	7½	10	18	20
1000	⅛	3	6½	8 ¾	15¾	17½
1030	⅓	2¼	5	6 ½	12	13¼
1100	½	1¾	3¾	5	9	10
1130	¾	¾	1¾	2½	4½	5
1200	No value	0	0	0	0	0

Figure 10. Wind discounts applied.

Other shooters memorize the full-value deflections for each range and then apply the appropriate "discount" to the value of the wind. For example, using the wind discounts applied chart (Figure 10):

- If the full-value deflection of a 20 mph wind at 1,000 yards is 20 MOA, then its deflection at 10 o'clock would be 20 MOA discounted by ⅛ (i.e., a deflection of 17½ MOA), and its deflection at 11 o'clock would be ½ of 20 MOA, or 10 MOA.

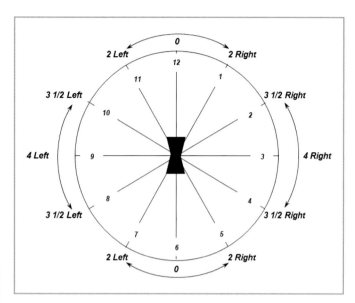

Figure 11. Wind behavior in quadrants.

Another way to look at this is shown in the wind behavior diagram (Figure 11). Here we can see that winds behave similarly from quadrant to quadrant. For example, a 3 o'clock wind and a 9 o'clock wind have the same value—only their directions are different. Therefore, if you need a 4 MOA right correction for a 4 mph wind from 3 o'clock, you will need a 4 MOA left correction for a 4 mph wind from 9 o'clock. Whether the wind is from behind or from in front (e.g., 8 o'clock or 10 o'clock) makes no difference to the amount of bullet deflection it will produce. Because of this symmetry between the quadrants, you need only learn the behavior of wind in one quadrant, and then you can apply it to all.

There is an interesting point to note about the behavior of the bullet when the wind crosses from one quadrant to another. When you are dealing with a fishtailing wind that is playing from 2 o'clock to 4 o'clock, you can expect to have a fairly small amount of deflection change as the wind fishtails. As shown in Figure 11, with a 4 mph wind and a 4 MOA right setting for the full-value (3 o'clock) correction, the correct sight setting for 2 and 4 o'clock would be 3½ MOA right.

To apply this to a target, Figure 12 shows three 1-minute circles inside of the bull. This diagram demonstrates what will happen if you put 3¾ minutes on your sight and shoot through the fishtailing conditions:

- The circle in the middle represents the group you could expect if you set your sight at 3¾ when the wind condition needed exactly that.
- The circle on the left represents the group you could expect if you set your sight at 3¾ when the wind condition really needed 3½.
- The circle on the right represents the group you could expect if you set your sight at 3¾ when the wind condition needed 4 minutes.

In every case, your shots would land well inside the bull. Therefore, when you have a switching wind of this type (switching between 2 and 4 o'clock) you could set your sight at 3¾ and shoot a string of bulls and V-bulls.[15]

However, when you are dealing with a fishtailing wind that is playing from 11 o'clock to 1 o'clock, it is a very different story. You can expect to have a significant amount of deflection change as the wind fishtails across the 12 o'clock position. With a 4 mph wind and a 4 MOA setting for the full value, you would need half-value left or 2 MOA left for the 11 o'clock wind, and 2 MOA right for the 1 o'clock wind. Figure 13 shows three 1-minute circles spread across a target face.

- The circle on the left represents the group you could expect if you set your sight at zero when the wind condition really needed 2 minutes right.
- The circle in the middle represents the group you could expect if you set your sight at zero when the wind condition needed exactly that.
- The circle on the right represents the group you could expect if you set your sight at zero when the wind condition needed 2 minutes left.

Therefore, a tactic of setting on the midpoint (i.e., in this case, setting your sight at zero and leaving it there) would prove disastrous, producing a string of many inners and magpies.

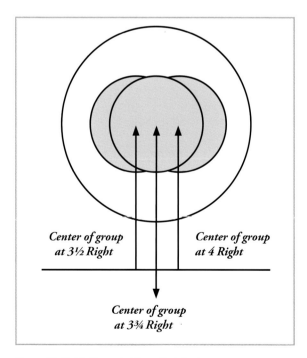

Center of group at 3½ Right

Center of group at 4 Right

Center of group at 3¾ Right

Figure 12. Fishtailing wind from 3 o'clock.

SCORING BASICS

The United States uses a decimal target system, with the score values at each ring being (from the center) 10, 9, 8, 7, and so on, with an X (roman numeral for 10) designating a special 10-value (used to break ties). For long-range shooting, the British (and therefore the Commonwealth countries) use a scoring system that values each ring (from the center) as 5, 4, 3, and so on, with a V (roman numeral for 5) designating a special 5-value (used to break ties). To add to the clarity of the scorer's calls during firing, each of these score values is given a descriptive to improve communications. So the scorer would call: V-bull, bull-five, inner-four, magpie-three, or outer-two. There are some additional local variations, such as the Aussies' use of the word "center" for V-bull.

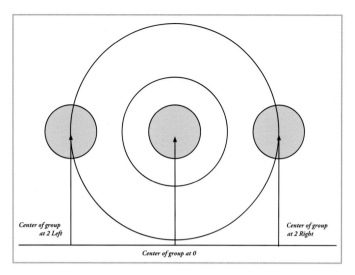

Figure 13. Fishtailing wind from 12 o'clock.

WHAT'S MORE IMPORTANT—WIND DIRECTION OR SPEED?

The truth is, it depends. Sometimes wind direction is more critical, and sometimes speed is more significant. Take a look at Figure 14, which shows approximate sight settings for 600 yards under various wind conditions.

The 1 o'clock column shows that for wind from this direction, each additional 4 mph of wind requires only 1 additional MOA correction. Therefore, with each noticeable increase in wind, you need add only a minute. If you're not sure about the increase and add only half a minute, you'll still get a bull. Even if you miss the wind increase altogether, odds are you'll get a bull at least 50 percent of the time.

	Speed	12 o'clock	1 o'clock	2 o'clock	3 o'clock
Very Strong	20 mph	0	5	8	10
Strong	16 mph	0	4	6½	8
Fresh	12 mph	0	3	5	6
Moderate	8 mph	0	2	3½	4
Gentle	4 mph	0	1	1½	2

Figure 14. Wind chart for 600 yards, highlighting speed vs. direction.

The 3 o'clock column shows that for wind from this direction, each additional 4 mph of wind requires a 2-minute correction. Therefore, an unnoticed wind increase will very

likely give you an inner. So, you can conclude that when you are shooting in winds from 3 o'clock, you need to be very aware of wind velocity.

Now let's look at the chart from the other way—what happens when the wind velocity is constant, but the angle is changing?

- If you look across the Gentle row—highlighted in the wind chart (Figure 15) below—you will see that a change in angle will only move you from one side of the bull to the other, and a sight setting of 1½ minutes will keep you happily in V-bulls and bulls.
- Take a look at the Fresh row, and you will see that there's another story here. A small shift from 1 o'clock to 2 o'clock (highlighted in Figure 15) will give you an inner, without batting an eye! This is one of the conditions that many shooters miss, to their peril.
- Even more deadly, however, is a change from 12 o'clock to 1 o'clock—in almost every case, you will get at least an inner—when the wind is very strong (highlighted in Figure 15) you will probably get a magpie for missing this wind change.

	Speed	12 o'clock	1 o'clock	2 o'clock	3 o'clock
Very Strong	20 mph	0	5	8	10
Strong	16 mph	0	4	6½	8
Fresh	12 mph	0	3	5	6
Moderate	8 mph	0	2	3½	4
Gentle	4 mph	0	1	1½	2

Figure 15. Wind chart for 600 yards, highlighting direction changes.

There's one other interesting phenomenon that our little chart demonstrates: several wind change combinations do not require a sight change. For example, as shown in Figure 16, a gentle wind from 3 o'clock and a moderate wind from 1 o'clock both require a 2-minute sight setting.

Notice, however, that in order to switch from 3 o'clock to 1 o'clock, the wind must pass through the 2 o'clock setting, which will require a setting of either 1½ minutes or 3½ minutes. If you are shooting with a 2-minute setting during that shift, you'll get a bull if you really needed the 1½ and an inner if you really needed the 3½ setting.

	Speed	12 o'clock	1 o'clock	2 o'clock	3 o'clock
Very Strong	20 mph	0	5	8	10
Strong	16 mph	0	4	6½	8
Fresh	12 mph	0	3	5	6
Moderate	8 mph	0	2	3½	4
Gentle	4 mph	0	1	1½	2

Figure 16. Wind chart for 600 yards, highlighting offsetting changes at low wind speeds.

	Speed	12 o'clock	1 o'clock	2 o'clock	3 o'clock
Very Strong	20 mph	0	5	8	10
Strong	16 mph	0	4	6½	8
Fresh	12 mph	0	3	5	6
Moderate	8 mph	0	2	3½	4
Gentle	4 mph	0	1	1½	2

Figure 17. Wind chart for 600 yards, highlighting offsetting changes at high wind speeds.

Let's look at one final example in Figure 17. A strong wind from 3 o'clock and a very strong wind from 2 o'clock both require an 8-minute correction. As long as the wind is switching favorably between these two conditions, you will be able to produce a very nice group with a single sight setting. However, if the wind starts to increase in angle before it lets off in velocity, you'll need 10 minutes to keep you out of the inner. Also, if the wind lets off and drops back to 2 o'clock, you'll need only 6½—if your sight is sitting at 10 minutes, you'll have a magpie!

MIRAGE

After flags, mirage is the next most commonly used wind indicator. Mirage is the sight of heat waves, which are usually present in hot climates and on hot days in temperate climates.[16] Mirage will be intermittent on a partly cloudy day. Mirage can sometimes be seen with the unaided eye but is best viewed with a scope—and the better the scope, the sooner you will be able to see mirage when it is forming or returning. (Some national teams are equipped with enormous scopes for the team matches, because they think that seeing the details of mirage—especially when there is very little of it around—is important competitive information.)

Mirage combines the effect of the speed of the wind with the angle of the wind and shows the shooter the total value of the wind. The direction of the ripples in the mirage indicates the wind direction (left or right). The number (frequency) and size (amplitude) of the ripples vary with wind force.

Because mirage has very little physical mass, it has very little inertia or momentum; so, it is very responsive to changes. The fact that mirage shows small wind changes makes mirage particularly useful during periods of gentle winds, which do not show well on the flags. The fact that mirage responds quickly and shows a wind change almost immediately makes it especially helpful during reversals (fishtailing winds that cross the 12 o'clock position).

As shown in Figure 18:

- When there is a headwind or tailwind, the mirage shimmers straight up and is said to be "boiling."
- At 1–3 mph, the mirage is no longer boiling straight up but is starting to show a direction; however, it is not yet flowing. Some people describe this as "leaning"; we usually describe it as "a boil, with a tendency from the left (or from the right)."
- At 4 mph, the mirage has flopped over and is flowing gently.
- At 8 mph, the mirage is flowing rapidly, and assessing changes may be getting difficult. Many shooters believe it is better to rely on flags—or at least to cross-reference the flag positions to the mirage—at this point.
- At 12 mph, the ripples are starting to disappear. The mirage is starting to show just a horizontal stream, which is also known as "flatlining."
- At 16 mph or more, the mirage usually disappears entirely.

Standard Description	Mph	Kph	Ft/ sec	Mirage Description	Mirage Diagram
	0-1	0-2	0-2	Boiling. Streamers flowing upwards with no lateral movement	
	1-3	2-5	2-4	Leaning. Mostly upward movement, but starting to "lean" enough to clearly depict direction of wind	
Gentle	4	6	6	Flowing gently. Clearly horizontal flow in big waves, moving loosely and slowly.	
Moderate	8	13	12	Flowing rapidly. Streamers flowing horizontally with small waves, close together.	
Fresh	12	19	18	Slick. Mirage streaming quickly. Difficult to see changes. Flatlining	
Strong	16	25	24	Mirage gone.	
Very Strong	20	32	29		

Figure 18. Mirage description chart.

Many shooters are concerned that mirage refracts the light, producing an image of the aiming mark that is displaced from its true location. Most experts disagree—at least in practical terms, at yards, they say that any displacement is negligible.[17] Still it is difficult for many shooters to learn to tolerate the shimmer, loss of definition, or sense of movement that the aiming mark takes on during heavy mirage. The image shimmers around the true position of the aiming mark. While you may need to increase the size of your front aperture, by simply relaxing and focusing your attention on firing a perfect shot, you can produce solid groups with iron sights.

Shooters using telescopic sights at long range in heavy mirage face a different set of problems. In general, the higher the magnification of the scope, the harder it is to see through the mirage to the aiming mark. In addition, if you aim off center and the aiming mark appears to be dancing around, you really cannot tell where your aim point is. The best choice in heavy mirage is to center the dancing mass of the aiming mark in the center of the scope. If your scope magnification is variable, you may find it easier to center this mass at a lower magnification.

UNDERSTANDING TIME IN FLIGHT

"It takes about two seconds for that rifle bullet to travel about a thousand yards . . . it takes *time* for the wind to act on the bullet, and only after quite a long time can the sideways motion of the bullet approach the sideways velocity of the moving air. At all other times, the bullet *must* (a) be moving sideways more slowly than the moving air, and (b) be speeding up sideways all the time the moving air is acting on it. In theory, in our styles of shooting, our bullets should never reach the lateral speed of the air that moves it."[18]

The Flight Path of the Bullet

One of the ways to start understanding the bullet's time in flight is to picture the flight path. Figure 19 shows an approximation of an average match-grade .308 bullet fired from about 1,000 yards.[19] This flight path is quite a lot like the flight path of a softball thrown underhand. There are some interesting features about this flight path.

The first thing that surprises many shooters is just how high the bullet flies. If your elevation setting at 1,000 yards is 40 MOA, then you have adjusted the line of departure to be 40 inches at 100 yards. If gravity did not act on the bullet, it would continue flying at that angle, and by the time it cleared the line of targets, it would be 400 inches (over 33 feet) above the line of sight. However, gravity is working on the trajectory of the bullet from the moment the bullet leaves the muzzle. Depending on the height of the flagpoles at your range, the bullet will usually fly near the height of the flags at its culminating (highest) point.

Another important aspect of this flight path is that the bullet leaves the "mirage zone" for most of its flight. The mirage zone is the area where you can see mirage, which is typically only a few feet off the ground (and limited by the area of view of your scope, as well as the background object you are using to get a clear view of the mirage, usually the target frame).

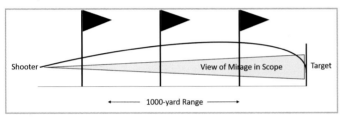

Figure 19. Trajectory and wind indicators diagram (approximation only, not to scale).

The shape of the flight path (a parabolic curve, or almost a teardrop shape) affects the time in flight. The farther the bullet flies in pure horizontal distance, its time in flight is proportionally greater because of the shape of its flight path. When there is also windage correction on the sights, the bullet's path not only sweeps up vertically, it also sweeps into the wind and therefore spends even more time in flight to achieve the straight-line distance to the target. And, although it doesn't show in the diagram, the bullet is slowing down as it moves downrange.

All these facts—and more—are taken into consideration in ballistics charts, which calculate elevation and windage requirements for a given bullet starting out from the muzzle at a specific velocity.

It is helpful to the shooter who wishes to understand wind reading to appreciate some of the complexities that go into the behavior of the bullet, in order to appreciate the deflection of the bullet in different wind conditions.[20]

Deflection

A wind will deflect a bullet throughout its flight, so its deflection becomes greater and greater as the bullet travels longer distances. In addition, the bullet is slowing down, and the distance traveled is increasing. You can use the information in reloading manuals and ballistics programs to calculate the correct values for your specific ammunition and load. Figure 20 shows the deflection of several classic and popular calibers with a 4 mph wind.

Starting at the lowest line, the graph shows the deflection of the extremely efficient 6.5mm-284 cartridge. Its deflection at 900 meters is about 2 minutes in a 4 mph crosswind.

The next line shows the deflection of the 6mm BR, another popular cartridge, which is particularly efficient considering its very light 107-grain Sierra bullet and fairly soft (easy to shoot) load. Note that at 900 meters, it requires almost 3 minutes of correction.

The next line shows the deflection of the very commonly used .308 bullet (155-grain Sierra). As you can see, at 900 meters, the deflection is almost double that of the most efficient caliber.

Figure 20. Deflection of common calibers at 4 mph.

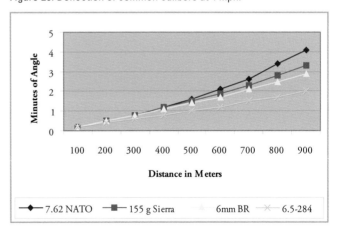

Finally, at the top, the 7.62mm NATO round is shown. This is the cartridge that most British wind tables are based on, and it is commonly the round used when a match is conducted with "issue ammunition." The 7.62 NATO is also the round upon which most wind-calling rules of thumb are based. The rule of thumb for an average-velocity .308 round is that for each mile per hour of crosswind, the bullet will be deflected 1 MOA at 1,000 yards. For example, a 4 mph crosswind will move the bullet 4 MOA at 1,000 yards, and a 20 mph crosswind will move the bullet 20 MOA at 1,000 yards.

Figure 21 shows the wind deflections given in most British resource materials. Note that the curve gets steeper as the distance increases. Therefore, you will notice that a 20 mph wind is deflected 20 MOA at 1,000 yards; however, the same wind at 500 yards (half the distance) moves the bullet one-third of the MOA. In fact, 50 percent of the effect of the wind (i.e., 10 MOA deflection caused by a 20 mph wind) occurs at about 650 yards.

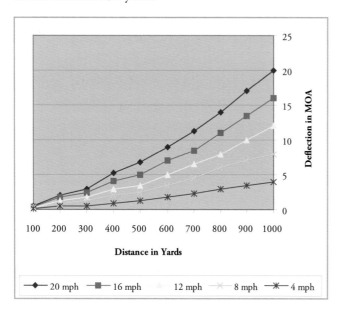

Figure 21. British wind calculator in graph format.

Now let us look at some real numbers. Figure 22 shows the real British Wind Calculator numbers. (The British Wind Calculator is a cardboard, pin-wheel-like device in common use among Commonwealth shooters. The user turns the pinwheel to reflect current wind conditions—speed and angle—and the appropriate MOA settings are shown in the cut-out window.) It is easy to see that the longer the bullet

	200	300	500	600	900	1000
20 mph	2	3	6¾	9	17	20
16 mph	1¾	2½	5	7	13½	16
12 mph	1¼	1¾	3½	5	10	12
8 mph	¾	1¼	2½	3½	7	8
4 mph	½	½	1¼	1¾	3½	4

Figure 22. British wind calculator in table format.

is in flight, the greater the correction that is required for a given wind condition. It is also important to note that the amount of deflection per 100 yards is greater the longer the bullet is in flight.

For example, a 20 mph wind requires 3 minutes of correction at 300 yards (an average of 1 minute per 100 yards for the first 300 yards); however, the next 300-yard segment (from 300 to 600 yards) requires 6 more minutes of correction (an average of 2 minutes per 100 yards for that segment) and the final 300 yards (from 700 to 1,000 yards) requires almost 9 more minutes of correction (an average of almost 3 minutes per 100 yards for that segment).[21]

This demonstrates the accumulating deflection that will become an important aspect of the near/far debate, discussed later in this chapter.

WIND BEHAVIOR

Wind conditions may be uniform (i.e., consistent in the length of the bullet's flight) or nonuniform (i.e., varying in strength or direction along the bullet's line of flight).

In wide-open spaces with no hills or obstacles, you can expect the wind to be fairly regular in velocity and direction. A flat, open field usually produces fairly uniform wind, while obstructions, hills, valleys, and tree lines usually produce nonuniform wind. Wind may be diverted or divided by obstacles. It may run in currents. It may roll or eddy or shear. Near large water, it may be windier, but it is often more uniform than in a wooded or hilly inland location.

Another consideration in assessing the uniformity of the wind is the stratification, or layers of wind, that may be present. At shorter ranges, the trajectory of the bullet does not rise above the top of the target frame, and so watching the mirage gives you a good picture of the air that your bullet will traverse. At longer ranges, the trajectory of the bullet rises above the ground-wind layer, and at 1000 yards, the average .308 bullet culminates more than 10 feet above the ground, and so watching the flags may give you a better picture of the air your bullet will traverse.

Because ground wind is slowed by friction with the ground, it is measurably slower than the wind in the upper air; in fact, the wind within 1 meter of the ground will typically travel about three-quarters as fast as the wind at 10 meters above the ground.

Many shorter ranges, and particularly smallbore ranges, are built in a bowl shape, where the wind slides down into the range in one corner, crosses the range floor diagonally, and exits at the other corner in an updraft, creating eddies in the opposite corners. This adds to the challenge and delight of making very subtle wind calls.

The real point, though, is that the shooter who wishes to master the wind needs to study it to truly understand and anticipate its behavior.

Uniform and Nonuniform Wind Conditions

"Wind is subject to two variations: (1) in strength, and (2) in direction. These changes may be uniform over the whole range or may be confined to parts of them. It is simpler to start with the changes that are uniform over the whole range and to leave the more complicated task till later."[22]

Our discussion so far has dealt with uniform wind conditions. The underlying assumption of all wind charts is that the wind is acting on the bullet from the same direction with the same force throughout its trajectory. This is rarely so.

	200 y	300 y	500 y	600 y	900 y	1000 y
20 mph	2	3	6¾	9	17	20

Figure 23. Wind chart for 20 mph at 200 yards to 1,000 yards.

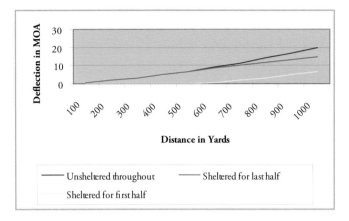

Figure 24. Deflection of sheltered bullets.

The fact is that the wind is rarely uniform. Therefore, you are usually using an approximation of all the wind conditions acting on the bullet during its flight.

The total effect of the wind is a result of three interdependent factors acting on the bullet:

- Distance traveled by the bullet
- Under what conditions (speed and direction)
- During which part of the flight

The question we get most often is, "Which are more important, the near flags or the far flags?" The answer is the near flags. The reason is that deflection initiated at the beginning of the trajectory is magnified over the entire flight, and the effect of this magnification is far greater than any new or changed conditions could completely counteract.

Let's look at a fairly simple situation. We are shooting at 1,000 yards with a 20 mph crosswind. Figure 23 shows the standard wind deflections for a 20-mph wind at 1,000 yards. We fire our shot with no wind correction and find that it lands 20 MOA downwind. This situation is represented by the top line on the graph in Figure 24.

Then, magically, a giant wall is erected, blocking all the crosswind from 500 to 1,000 yards. We then fire another shot. For the first 500 yards, the crosswind acts on the bullet, deflecting it 6¾ minutes. From then on, there is no wind acting on the bullet, and the bullet continues to fly toward the target, at the angle established before the wind stopped blowing on it. This is represented by the middle line on the graph in Figure 24.

Then, again magically, the giant wall is moved, so that now the wind is blocked for the first 500 yards and blows freely on the bullet for the next 500 yards. This is represented by the bottom line on the graph in Figure 24.

It is easy to see, in this small example, that the wind blowing on the bullet early in its flight establishes a course that will largely determine its total deflection.

If the force varies during the flight of the bullet, it is the first wind that the bullet encounters that will have the greatest effect. As Figure 24 demonstrates:

- A bullet that receives the full force of the wind throughout its flight will be deflected the most; about 20 minutes in our example.
- One that receives the full force of the wind for the first half of its flight, and then is sheltered for the latter half, is deflected about 6¾ minutes in the first half and then follows that line of flight, resulting in a total deflection of almost 15 minutes by the time the bullet has reached the target.
- One that receives full sheltering for the first half of the flight, and then is subjected to the full force of the wind, will be deflected considerably less; about 7 minutes in total in our example.

Recall our discussion earlier, where we noted that the amount of deflection of the bullet grows significantly as it travels through the 1,000-yard flight. Our example was a 20 mph wind, and we noted that the deflection would be:

- 3 minutes at 300 yards (an average of 1 minute per 100 yards)
- 6 more minutes for the next 300 yards (from 300 to 600 yards; an average of 2 minutes per 100 yards)
- 9 more minutes for the final 300 yards (from 700 to 1,000 yards; an average of almost 3 minutes per 100 yards)

The reason the bullet is deflected more in the last 300 yards of travel than in the first 300 yards of travel is largely because the deflection acquired during its flight is cumulative.

If you need more convincing, or just want more information, take a look at the following near/far debate.

Near/Far Debate

The relative values of near and far flags have been addressed mathematically by the likes of Des Burke and Robin Fulton, and more recently updated by Raymond Von Wahlde and John C. Simpson (in *Tactical Shooter* magazine). Even so, we have found that in some quarters, the debate continues.

Below, we give a summary of the near/far debate.

A lot has been written about the value of the near wind versus the value of the far wind. This much is known:

- Deflection is an angular effect. That is to say, the earlier in a bullet's flight that it is deflected, the greater is its displacement at the target; therefore the wind nearest to the shooter will cause the greatest deflection.
- Later in the trajectory, the bullet velocity has slowed and now will give the wind more time to influence its flight path, but it is now very close to the target, and the opportunity for deflection is decreasing.

The basis of the debate is whether the early deflection can be overcome or offset by the later increased time in flight. And the answer is yes, but rarely. The more usual circumstance is that the path determined by early deflection is modified, but not determined, by the far winds. The clear exceptions are the following:

- The bullet is sheltered during the first part of its flight, and only the far wind acts on it, in which case the shooter would use a wind chart for the distance that the wind is acting on the bullet.[23]
- The near wind is gentle and the far wind is extreme, and the difference required to have an effect would not normally occur in nature.[24]

Under most normal wind conditions, the usual rule is that the near flags are determinants and the far flags are modifiers.

What Others Say about "Near or Far"

Having now researched this topic from many sources, we are not sure why it is still being debated—the overwhelming majority of sources indicate that it is without question the wind nearer the shooter that has the greatest effect on the trajectory of the bullet.[25] However, for those who are still discussing this topic on the range, here are some of the opinions and facts that we have uncovered.

From *Target Rifle Shooting* by E.G.B. Reynolds and Robin Fulton:

Reynolds and Fulton note that not everyone understands why the flags closer to the shooter are more important wind indicators than the flags closer to the target, and that people sometimes think that because the bullet speed is dropping as it progresses toward the target it will be more likely to be affected by the wind at that end of the range. "The explanation is that once a bullet is deflected from its course by wind, it does not recover its initial direction, even if no wind affects the latter part of its flight."

From *Highpower Rifle* by G. David Tubb:

David Tubb writes that while most of the ranges in his experience have fairly uniform wind, sometimes the conditions vary on the length of the range. And while he

acknowledges that there is some debate about whether it is the wind at the shooter end of the range or the wind at the target end of the range that has the greater effect, he maintains, "Without question, wind closer to the shooter has more effect. The reason is that the bullet will be deflected earlier; the farther it travels, the farther off path it strays."

From *Canadian Bisley Shooting* by Desmond T. Burke:

"If there is a uniform wind condition of 10 minutes, and a flag change to what would be 7 minutes if it occurred over the entire range . . . obviously the actual wind requirement must be between the upper limit of 10 and a lower limit of 7 . . . [If the let-off is on the near flags, then] the shooter should reduce the wind allowance to about 8 minutes . . . [If the let-off is on the far flags, then] a change of sight to 9 minutes would be a reasonable approximation.

"[T]he starting point is always—what wind would one allow if the wind for a segment prevailed over the whole range? And average that with the same conjectures regarding the other segment."[26]

From "Kentucky Windage Goes High-Tech: Development of a Laser Crosswind Sensor" by Raymond Von Wahlde in *Tactical Shooter*, March 1999:

"[Even though the bullet is slowing down as it moves downrange, and spending more time in the down-range wind] bullets tend to be more sensitive to crosswind that they experience nearer the shooter than the same cross-wind closer to the target [measured by total deflection at the target] . . . For any given bullet deflection at a particular range, there are an infinite number of intervening cross-wind profiles (only one of which is a constant, uniform wind) that would result in the same deflection. It is this effective cross-wind profile that a shooter . . . is tasked with determining."

From "Wind Reading—Another Way of Looking at It?" by Charles F. Young in *Tactical Shooter*, April, 1998:

"[F]ired with any crosswind blowing . . . our bullet is deflected from the path we carefully chose for it . . . and it adopts a sideways velocity, which it will tend to retain even if the wind drops further down the range. If the wind keeps blowing on the bullet, the bullet's lateral velocity will increase until it eventually approaches wind-speed. [The wind drift of] an average 30-cal. 155 grain bullet fired at 2,900 fps [will be] around 108 inches at 1,000 yards if it is blown throughout by a 10 mph (15 fps) wind . . . If the bullet took . . . 1.6 seconds to travel 1,000 yards, how come the drift is more than FIVE TIMES as much? The answer is that the bullet's sideways velocity is increasing all the way down the range, as the wind keeps pressing on it."

From "The Question Is Blowin' in the Wind" by John C. Simpson in *Tactical Shooter*, August 2000:

"If you stay in the long-range shooting game long enough you'll eventually hear the following question: 'Where does the wind have the most effect on the bullet's path?' The 'downrange wind' gang would theorize that because the bullet was traveling slower, the wind closest to the target would have more of an effect in pushing it to the side . . . This article will explain how to figure the relative effectiveness of winds that are blowing across only a part of the range (or nonuniform) . . . step by step until we have calculated the downrange deflection of a bullet influenced by the wind in 100 yard increments. [For example] a bullet path moved by a uniform wind of 10 mph blowing across the full range [is deflected 110 inches or 10.5 MOA] . . . if we build a very high wall to block the wind from the 500 yard line to the thousand . . . the bullet is deflected about 22 inches at 500 yards [and at] the 1,000 yard mark reveals a deflection of about 73 inches . . . The third [example] shows the wind blocking wall extending from the muzzle to 500 yards . . . [which results in a total deflection] of 37 inches at 1,000 yards.[27]

"A ten mile per hour wind blowing from three o'clock at 0–100 yards will deflect the bullet about 15 inches at 1,000 yards. A nine o'clock wind blowing at 900–1,000 yards would have to have a speed of about 80 miles per hour to push a bullet 15 inches! A wind from the opposite direction between 600 and 700 yards would have to be traveling . . . 13.6 miles per hour."

And the sole dissenting voice on this matter:

From *Advanced Rifle Training* by the FBI Academy Firearms Training Unit:

In *Advanced Rifle Training*, the FBI instructs that "the wind deflection is minimal close to the shooter, and maximal at the target." This manual goes on to say that the shooter should read the wind (speed and direction) about two-thirds to three-quarters of the way to the target, and base his sight correction on that reading. The authors of this advice are clearly putting more importance on the slowing of the bullet than the initial angle of deflection.

Let's Get Practical

In fact, once the shooter understands the basic idea that under most normal circumstances, the near wind determines the deflection and the far wind can offset it, but only marginally, there are some practical ways of dealing with nonuniform wind.

The first situation to address is the uniform wind condition:

- When all the flags are showing one uniform condition, the value shown in your wind chart for that distance is probably correct (or at least it is a good place to start).

The next situation to deal with is the nonuniform condition:

- When the far flags (at the target end of the range) drop or rise in value (either by velocity or direction changes), there will be a slightly different total wind deflection on your bullet.

And now comes the practical part:

- When the near flags change value, start using your wind chart for that new value, and modify it slightly upward or downward to accommodate the behavior of the far flags.

In other words, always use the near flags to decide what the condition is and then modify your assessment of it depending on what the far flags are doing.

Let's look at an example for conditions at 600 yards. As shown in Figure 25:

- If the flags show a uniform 20 mph crosswind throughout the length of the range, you would expect 9 minutes of deflection.
- If the flags show a uniform 16 mph crosswind throughout the length of the range, you would expect 7 minutes of deflection.

You know that any nonuniform condition that has a mixture of 16 and 20 mph indicators would result in deflection between 7 and 9 minutes.

	100	200	300	400	500	600
20 mph	0.5	2.0	3.0	5.25	6.75	9.0
16 mph	0.4	1.75	2.5	4.17	5.0	7.0
12 mph	0.3	1.25	1.75	2.92	3.5	5.0
8 mph	0.2	0.75	1.25	2.08	2.5	3.5
4 mph	0.1	0.5	0.5	0.92	1.25	1.75

Figure 25. Wind chart from 100 yards to 600 yards.

And you know that the near flags are the key determining factor, so:

- If the near flags are at 16 mph and the far flags are at 20 mph, you would expect to see just a little more deflection than 7 minutes, perhaps 7½ or 7¾.

- If the near flags are at 20 mph and the far flags are at 16 mph, you would expect to see just a little less deflection than 9 minutes, perhaps 8¼ or 8½.

In practical terms then, at 600 yards, you would make your wind call based on the near flags and then modify the call up or down slightly to accommodate the behavior of the far flags. In fact, for target rifle competition, the bull is so large (2 minutes wide approximately) that a ½-minute correction on a change in the far flags is well within the standard required.

At 1,000 yards the same technique applies, but it does become a little trickier. The difference between a "strong" and a "very strong" wind at 1,000 yards is 4 minutes (16 MOA and 20 MOA).

On most targets, the bull is about 2 MOA wide. Therefore, you must make an accurate assessment of the relative value of the near and far conditions in order to stay in the bull. We will cover this situation and several further tactics for dealing with nonuniform conditions in chapter 3, "Techniques and Tactics."

Drift

Because the bullet spins as it moves through the air, it is subject to a slight gyroscopic effect. The standard target rifle with clockwise rifling imparts a clockwise spin on the bullet, and this spin gradually moves the bullet to the right as it flies forward. Over a distance of 1,000 yards (for a .308 bullet), the total effect is about 1 minute of angle. The only time it is really noticeable is when you are faced with a wind that switches on each side of 12 o'clock at long range; otherwise (with the wind from one side or another) the effect tends to disappear within our wind estimate.

Serious target rifle competitors will often use an alternate rear sight for long range. This sight will have a windage zero that incorporates wind drift, so that when there is no wind, the sight reads "zero," and in a switching wind the sight moves across the zero setting exactly as the shooter would expect.

Setting Your Sights

Wind from the left moves your bullet right. Therefore, we add left windage to compensate for its effect. It is very important that you refer to wind from the left as "left wind" so that you can consistently think of "left wind" requiring "left-wind correction"—i.e., moving your sights to the left. (If you start down the path of thinking about where the wind is going or where the bullet would go if its path were not changed by a sight setting, you will get yourself hopelessly tied up in which way is left or right on your sight.)

There are two primary ways to compensate for wind deflection: adjust your sights or aim off. As a general rule, we advocate making the sight adjustment rather than aiming off. Which you choose may depend on your equipment and your shooting preferences.

- With sights that do not adjust for windage (e.g., some service rifles): aim off.
- With aperture sights (e.g., target rifle): adjust the rear sight.
- With a telescopic sight with target turrets (fully adjustable): adjust the windage knob. (Many shooters aim off to compensate for changes seen in the mirage during aiming, but this must be done with care, because the mirage you see in your sight is at the target end of the range.)

Whether you aim off or adjust your sight can also vary by the type of match you are shooting.

- If you are shooting single string (you fire your string of shots on your own time without interruption), you can choose between aiming off and adjusting your sights.
- If your single string match is a snap fire or a rapid fire, you will probably have to aim off to accommodate match timings.
- If you are shooting alternately (you fire in turn with two or three other shooters on the same target, also known as "Bisley style"), you will probably need to keep careful

records, and adjusting your sights makes the record keeping easier and more accurate.

Some shooters, especially those with high-power telescopic sights, aim off so that they have a smaller or clearer aiming mark than the center of the big aiming black on the target. This works for many people, as long as the matches are short in duration and the winds are relatively stable. When the match takes a long time and the winds change often, the shooter may have to mix sight changes and aim point changes, and then cannot always remember and quickly analyze the results each got. Furthermore, at longer ranges with heavier mirage, the shooter with the telescopic sight can sometimes do no more than the shooter with the aperture sight: center the shimmering, dancing mass that the aiming mark appears to become.

Making a Sight Correction

It is essential that you make the correct sight adjustment; that is, that you put on the sight the correction you want.[28] The most common error that shooters make is to turn the sights in the wrong direction. This needlessly costs points, often for several shots, until the error is discovered and the shooter gets "back in the rhythm" with the wind.

This problem is aggravated by the technology available to shooters. Some sights turn clockwise to add right wind, and some sights turn counterclockwise to add right wind. If you use both types of sights on different rifles, it is easy to forget yourself and turn the knobs the wrong way.

To ensure that you turn your sights the right way every time, here are some suggestions.

1. Make sure you can clearly and easily read your sight settings.
   - If you are using a telescopic sight, buy or make improved turret scales so that you are always certain what you have set on your sight.
   - If you are using vernier scale, carry a small magnifying glass with you.

2. Make sure you have a reminder that will ensure that you turn the sight in the correct direction.
   - ○ Put a diagram of the knob on your shooting diary page or on your Plot-o-Matic (EZ-Graf).[29]
   - ○ Mark a turning arrow on your sight.

SUMMARY

To understand wind reading, the shooter must be aware of the facts about ballistics and wind behavior and the relationship between them. When we discussed these subjects with many shooters, the following facts often came as a surprise.

- The typical flight path of a .308 bullet launched from 1,000 yards rises about the height of a one-story building.
- Wind flags are made of different materials, and the shooter needs to "calibrate" the flags at each range he visits.
- Wind is always referred to in terms of the direction it is coming from (so that left wind requires left windage correction).

- Wind from 11 o'clock has half the lateral force of a crosswind of the same velocity.
- When dealing with a headwind or a tailwind, pay most attention to wind direction; when dealing with a crosswind, pay most attention to wind velocity.
- While they may focus their attention on one or the other, most experienced shooters use both flags and mirage when both are present.
- The wind near the shooter has more effect on the ultimate shot fall of the bullet than the far wind has, purely because of the angular deflection it causes.
- The bullet drift caused by its spinning is really minimal and not noticeable at short and medium distances. At 1,000 yards, it is about 1 minute of angle, noticeable in a headwind when there is otherwise no lateral deflection.
- Making sight adjustments correctly is a challenge in itself and is the cause of a large number of windage errors during practices and matches.

CHAPTER 2

THE THOUGHT PROCESS

George Stidworthy, writing in *Rifle* magazine, emphasized the need for the shooter to carefully observe all the wind indicators and combine this information with an "objective appraisal of the results of the last shot."[1] This ability to focus on the indicators in detail is echoed throughout the writings of wind-reading experts. The ability to assess the results of the last shot in a dispassionate way is an equally important skill. The shooter needs to follow a logical process of observation and assessment, with no interference from the distractions that an emotional reaction to the outcome of a shot can produce.

In running our courses and teaching many shooters how to read the wind, we have found that very few shooters follow a logical, step-by-step process. Some have a process but are not aware of it, and so they apply it inconsistently. Most make a series of guesses, making virtually every shot a sighter. Some just go off their last shot, resulting in their chasing conditions and chasing errors.

The purpose of this overall procedure and thought process is to help the shooter develop a consistent method of "wind thinking" and decision making. There are two parts to the thought process.

1. The first part helps you to develop a game plan for this shoot and to come to a decision about the sight setting you will use to fire your first shot.[2] This procedure prior to the first shot of the match is extensive. It requires an assessment of the range facility, an estimation of the conditions, and a game plan for the match, as well as picking the sight setting you will use for your first sighter.
2. Following the first shot of a given match, the procedure focuses on identifying changes, and for each subsequent shot you have more and better data on which to base your decisions.

FOR YOUR FIRST SIGHTER

Step 1: Observe Conditions

If the range is new to you, you should visit it several times to observe conditions prior to the first time you have an opportunity to fire on it. Find out whether the range is situated in a location that would affect the wind conditions, such as near a body of water. Try to picture where the predominant wind would enter the range, and then picture other possible wind directions. Notice whether there are any barriers (man-made or natural) that would affect the wind. Look at the lay of the land to see if the topography would affect the flow of the wind as it crosses the range floor. Notice if there are any windbreaks along the edges of the range. Look for wind indicators—the flags or flora that would likely provide an accurate reading of conditions you will need to shoot.

On match day, it is absolutely necessary to arrive at your firing point at least 20 to 30 minutes early. Get all the administration out of the way (target assignment, etc.), get lined up behind your firing point, and start analyzing the wind. You are looking to come to two conclusions:

1. What is my game plan for this shoot?
2. What is my initial sight setting for my first shot?

Here are some of the things you need to consider:[3]

- Decide on the flags you are going to use: for direction, one flag blowing directly at you or directly away from you; and for speed, one or more flags that are upwind and blowing at 90 degrees to your line of sight. Study these flags, memorizing their positions relative to the poles they are attached to, or to some distant horizon or tree line.
- Get your wind meter out and start watching the speed.
- Look for the high and low speeds and values to establish the bookends.

- Get your scope out and study the mirage. Look at it near the firing line, at midrange, and at the targets. Study how the mirage compares to the flags.
- Decide on the primary condition, and memorize what it looks like on the flags.
- Determine what the secondary condition is, and memorize what it looks like on the flags.
- Run a stopwatch to determine how long the primary condition lasts and, when the condition changes, record how long it takes to return to the primary condition.

Pat Vamplew is a double-gold Pan Am medalist, as well as a champion with many other shooting accomplishments. He is also a world-class wind reader and is well known for showing up at the firing point at least one relay ahead, with spotting scope and lawn chair in hand, to study the conditions.

David Tubb uses a similar tactic. He uses his stopwatch to mark the arrival of a significant condition change and then waits to see how long it takes for the cycle to change and return. He watches the cycle: the wind builds up, peaks, drops off, bottoms out, and then builds up again. He times the duration of the cycle, he says, "so I can anticipate these big changes."[4]

Charles F. Young advises: "Look for where points are being *lost*. Is that all around the aiming marks, or is it predominantly left and right? The latter tends to suggest rapidly changing wind speeds, but the former suggests steady winds."[5]

"This all falls in the category of reconnaissance, and we know that time spent on that is never wasted."[6]

Step 2: Convert Conditions to Sight Settings

Now that you fully understand what the conditions look like, start converting the conditions to measurements that you can use to set your sights. Start with your observations of the flags, the mirage, and the other objects, as well as the wind speed that you measured with your wind meter. Talk to other shooters and ask them what they are thinking about the wind. Watch the current relay of shooters, and when the wind whips up to the maximum bookend (or lets off to the minimum bookend), see if you can get an idea, from their shot placement, just how much wind change there was. Use charts and your previous shooting records to identify the value in minutes of your bookends, your primary condition, and your secondary condition.

The wind-patterning diagram (Figure 26) represents a fishtailing wind pattern that varies from a maximum bookend of 4 minutes of left wind to a maximum bookend of 3 minutes of right wind. The primary condition is about 1 minute left, and there is a short secondary condition of about 2 minutes right. One whole cycle takes about 12 minutes of time, with the left-wind build taking about 8 or 9 minutes of time. The mean is close to 0, but the wind spends almost no time there.

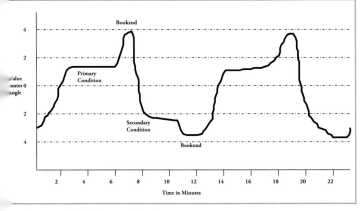

Figure 26. Wind-patterning diagram.

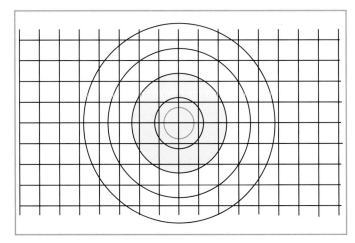

Figure 27. A 1,000-yard replica, 16 MOA wide.

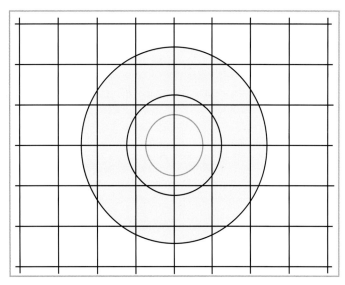

Figure 28. A 1,000-yard replica, 8 MOA wide.

Once you have a pretty clear picture of what the wind conditions are, you need to think about how you are going to deal with them.

- Decide on the mean sight setting for your shoot and set up your graph or Plot-o-Matic (EZ-Graf).[7]
- Choose the plotting diagram that's right for the conditions.

Figures 27 and 28 are both for use with a standard British 1,000-yard bull's-eye target.

- The first plotting diagram covers about 16 minutes of windage. This diagram makes it easier to plot when you are dealing with widely varying wind conditions. It also tends to help the timid shooter make bold sight changes.
- The second diagram covers about 8 minutes of windage. It makes it easier to plot your shots when they are clustered mostly in the bull and the V-bull. This diagram encourages the shooter to make the fine adjustments appropriate in gentler or steadier conditions.

"[T]ry to make up your mind before you shoot how you will categorize the wind. Is it across the range, or is it ahead or behind, and if so is it fishtailing? Each will best be handled by a slightly different strategy."[8] This part of the thought process will help you select the replica you will use (coarse or fine detail) and how you will set up your Plot-o-Matic (EZ-Graf) for windage (what the median wind condition is).

"By the time his squad is called, [the shooter] should have developed a plan of action that will enable him to approach the match with more confidence."[9]

Step 3: Make Your Wind Call and Set Your Sights

Once you are on the line and it is approaching your turn to fire your first shot, confirm your wind call and make sure your sight is correctly set. You have only one or two sighters (depending on the match rules) and you must get as much information as possible from them. Anticipate what the wind will be when you will be firing and fire the shot as quickly as you can fire a perfect shot. Firing quickly will minimize the chances of the wind changing while you are in the aim. If the wind is changing quickly, or if you have taken more than 10 seconds to fire, be prepared to hold your shot and glance at the flags or check the mirage in your spotting scope to see if the wind is still what you thought it was. If it is the same, then fire the shot quickly and accurately. If it has changed, make the sight adjustment and fire quickly and accurately.

Step 4: Fire and Call the Shot

It is essential that you fire a perfect shot and that you are completely confident that it is as perfect as you can fire—otherwise you will be corrupting the data you can get from this first sighter. "If one becomes too engrossed in theory and calculations, then poor holding, aiming, and firing will spoil one's score more than errors in wind judging."[10]

When we are teaching our police sniper students to fire a perfect shot under stress, we emphasize the need to separate themselves mentally from everything before they begin their mental program leading to the firing of a perfect shot. You can't think two things at once, and a perfect shot demands your full attention.

As soon as you have completed your follow-through, mentally call your shot, without prejudice. If you do not have this critical skill (being able to call your shot), you need to learn it—otherwise you will not be able to separate shot errors from wind effects. Then look at the flags and mirage and determine whether there were any wind changes during your shot execution that would have affected your shot placement.

Many of the sources we have researched emphasize the need for honesty in calling the shot; we believe that you must learn to have a dispassionate (nonemotional) attitude that focuses on the information you are getting and disregards entirely how you feel about your results while you are engaged in the match.

Step 5: Record and Analyze Results

When your target comes up with the shot indicator, record your shot placement on your graph or Plot-o-Matic (EZ-Graf) replica.

- If you called a center shot and your wind call was correct and the wind did not change while you were in the aim and the shot indicator is in the center (within your grouping capability), then you can say that all went well. All things being equal, you can carry on.
- Otherwise, you need to analyze the results and make sure you attribute any discrepancies to the correct cause.
  - If you called your shot low right and it is in fact low right, you know that your wind setting was correct; you just need to focus on firing perfect shots.
  - If you think you fired a perfect shot and expected the indicator to be in the center, but it is one minute left, then you have missed your wind call. Immediately adjust your windage based on shot placement before analyzing for your next shot. This recalibrates your thinking and reestablishes your baseline.

FOR SUBSEQUENT SHOTS

Step 6: Do Your Post-Shot Duties
Complete your post-shot work as quickly as possible; that is, record your shot placement, make sight adjustments for elevation and to center the group, record your score, and reload. As Reynolds and Fulton wrote in *Target Rifle Shooting,* the shooter must make corrections to center the group (and these may well be very small corrections) and make corrections for wind, when there is an observable change in wind speed or direction, but one type of correction should not be confused with the other.[11]

Our standard practice is to center the current condition on the Plot-o-Matic (EZ-Graf) and set our sights accordingly. Then we watch the wind.

Step 7: Assess Wind Changes
Keep your eye on your flags or on the mirage, and watch for wind changes. Soon you will have to decide on another wind call, and you want all the available information. To help get you thinking the right thoughts, ask yourself these questions to help lead you to the best decision.

1. "Is the wind the same or different?" If it is the same, do not make a sight adjustment—go with your corrected last shot. If it is different, this leads to another question.
2. "Has the wind increased in value or decreased?" Answering this question requires you to look at both velocity and direction. Your answer determines which way you will be turning your sight. "Always move the sight in the right direction even if you aren't sure how much to do it."[12]
3. "Is the change a little or a lot?" If you think it is a little, remember that it is difficult for the average person to see less than a 1-minute change at long range (except when watching a mirage go to and from a boil). If you think you see a change, it is at least a minute; if you are sure you see a change, it will be at least 2 minutes. You need to be aware of your own abilities and learn just what you can see.

"[I]f a shooter's experience indicates that he can judge wind changes at the shorts only when of the order of half a minute or more, he should realize that this corresponds to detecting a change of the order of about 2 minutes at 1,000. This is not an attempt to discredit those who make smaller changes at long ranges. Such changes are often necessary in the interest of group centering, and in light winds they can be judged from indicators. This is particularly true in the fishtail type of wind where a shooter may see changes of 1 minute or even less at 1,000 yards, though he may not detect changes in the indicators of less than 2 or 3 minutes in strong winds from 9 o'clock."[13]

- If only velocity has changed (direction is still the same), you probably have a modest change in a headwind, and you may have a significant change in a crosswind.
- If only direction has changed (velocity is still the same), you probably have a modest change in a crosswind, and you may have a significant change in a headwind or tailwind.
- If both velocity and direction have changed (one increased and the other decreased), you have a complex situation, one that few shooters respond well to. See the "Tools and Techniques" section for the sandbox technique. Briefly, there are four possible situations you must consider.
  - If both velocity and direction have increased the value of the wind, you know you have a very significant change.
  - If both velocity and direction have decreased the value of the wind, you know you have a very significant change. If the change is a lot, you may have to refer to your bookend settings to see how much adjustment to make. Under these circumstances you must be bold. As the saying goes, "An inner on one side is the same value as an inner on the other side." Memorize the flags and mirage for this extreme shot, and learn what the sight setting is for this condition—you will probably get it again.

o If velocity has increased and direction has decreased (or vice versa) the value of the wind, the net effect depends on the specific example, but, generally speaking,

—In a headwind or tailwind the direction change affects wind value more than the speed does; and

—In a crosswind the speed change affects wind value more than direction does.

o Sometimes, the direction and speed changes offset each other, and the net effect on the wind value is nil.

Let's look at some specific examples. Figure 29 is a wind chart showing the deflection at various wind speeds and directions.

- Say we are shooting with a 12 mph wind coming from 1 o'clock; we would expect 6 minutes of deflection. Since this is more a headwind than a crosswind, we would expect direction changes to be more significant than velocity changes. Sure enough, a wind blowing at the same speed from 12 o'clock will not deflect the bullet at all, and that's a 6-minute difference.

- The same velocity wind blowing from 3 o'clock deflects the bullet 12 minutes, but if the angle drops off to 2 o'clock, the deflection drops by only 1½ minutes. However, if that 3 o'clock wind picks up in velocity (to 16 mph) it will push the bullet an additional 4 minutes.

- If a strong headwind drops in speed and comes around from the side, it can end up with the same deflection. (For example, a 16 mph wind from 1 o'clock and 8 mph wind from 3 o'clock both produce 8 minutes of deflection.) However, this challenging situation can move through some very different deflections, depending on what mix of speed and direction is present at a given moment.

If you have ever felt a little overwhelmed by the conditions, it is probably in this latter situation. It is genuinely difficult to deal with, and we offer some strategies in chapter 4, "Techniques and Tactics."

Direction / Speed	Head wind	From 1 o'clock	From 2 o'clock	From 3 o'clock
4 mph	0	2	3½	4
8 mph	0	4	7	8
12 mph	0	6	10½	12
16 mph	0	8	14	16
20 mph	0	10	17½	20

Figure 29. Wind chart (speed and direction) for 1,000 yards.

Step 8: Make Decision, Set Sights, Fire Shot

- Always call your shot and make allowances for a less-than-perfect shot.
- Continue to observe the conditions as compared to what you know.
- Memorize the flags and/or mirage, so that you can recognize the condition as being the same or having changed.
- Talk to yourself. For example: "When the flag was like that, I used this sight setting and I got a bull"; or "The last time the flag was like that, I needed 7 minutes"; or "This wind is clearly outside the high bookend; I will need to go to 15 minutes." Many top shooters draw little pictures on their plotting diagrams to help them accurately observe and recall the indicators for specific conditions.

The more shots you've fired, the more information you have from which to make further decisions. If you get in trouble or there is a major wind change that you have not seen before, go back to the procedure for your first sighter.

SUMMARY

For Your First Sighter
- To determine your game plan for this shoot and

To determine your initial sight setting for your first shot:

Step 1: Observe conditions.

Step 2: Convert conditions to sight settings.

Step 3: Make your wind call and set your sights.

Step 4: Fire and call the shot.

Step 5: Record and analyze results; recalibrate your thinking as required.

For Subsequent Shots

- To determine your sight setting for your next shot:

  Step 6: Do your post-shot duties.

  Step 7: Assess wind changes.

    - Is the wind the same or different?

    - Has the wind increased in value or decreased?

    - Is the change a little or a lot?

  Step 8: Make your decision, set your sights, and fire your shot.

CHAPTER 3

TECHNIQUES AND TACTICS

"My first sighter was a bull with 4 minutes of wind, and my second sighter was a bull with 5 minutes of wind. I played the next shot for a V-bull, and lost the call. . . . I lost the point. I played the next several, trying to get V-bulls, and shot only bulls. Somewhere during that sequence, I realized that we had only 1-minute variation in the wind. I thought about the odds of calling the changes correctly (can I really perceive a half-minute of wind at 1,000 yards correctly to get the shot centered nicely in the V-bull?) or should I just set the sights for the mean of the wind settings and shoot perfect shots until something changes?

"I decided that I could stand to have fewer V-bulls, as long as I got the points. I set my sights for the mean wind condition and settled in to shoot perfect shots. The mirage was not reliable, so I was watching flags to make sure that nothing changed in the conditions that would require a change in strategy. I was particularly interested in one of the flags that was not quite halfway downrange. It was quite sensitive, it seemed—possibly because it was one of the few flags that did not have any trees or berms protecting it from the wind conditions. It would dance around quite a bit, but the angle did not really change much unless there was a real condition change. And the best indicator for what the condition changes were (when there were any) was the red safety flag on the top of the backstop—a little hard to see accurately at 1,000 yards, but it seemed very truthful.

"There were several times that I would have changed my sight setting if it had been my turn to shoot. But by the time it was my turn again, my key flag was back to its flippant little dance, and the condition was back to 'my condition.'

"I'm not sure whether it takes more courage to change your sights or to leave them alone. When I first started in this long-range game, I used to challenge myself to make the changes. The first few bold changes really took courage. But I had gotten over it in South Africa, where all the changes had to be bold. This match was a different story. It took a great deal of self-discipline to leave the sights alone.

"I finished the match without dropping another point and, while I picked up only three V-bulls, I was well satisfied with a score of 74 out of 75 at 1,000 yards."[1]

The starting point for developing your skills in wind reading is to acquire the fundamental observation and recording techniques that the top competitors use. The first part of this chapter focuses on techniques for reading flags and mirage effectively, using wind charts and wind diagrams, and recording and analyzing your own shooting data.

The next big step to develop your wind-reading effectiveness is to start to collect the set of tactics that will be part of your wind-reading toolbox. The simple act of identifying and recognizing these tactics will set you apart from the majority of shooters. Treating them like tools to be used as conditions dictate (much as a golfer chooses a club for the particular situation) will put you in a league of your own.

FLAG READING

Other than natural objects, there are two key things used to observe the wind: the flags and the mirage.

Flag reading is an art in itself, and art develops with practice. But there are two underlying skills that are so fundamental that you cannot progress without them.

- The single most important thing to understand about reading flags is that you must read two flags: one for direction and one for speed.
- The next most important thing you need to be able to do is interpret a field of flags that are describing nonuniform conditions.

"Sometimes one hears the term 'master flag.' In a uniform wind, any flag in the open will give accurate information, whether it is 50 or 1,000 yards away. Subsequent considerations of nonuniform winds may tempt a shooter to consider the near flag as the master flag, but he will see that even this is not completely true."[2]

Reading Two Flags

You must read a minimum of two flags: one to tell you the direction of the wind, and one to tell you the velocity of the wind, as shown in Figure 30.

The reason you need two flags is purely visual:

- To read wind direction, it is best that the flag point directly away or toward you, so that you can more easily see any changes.
- To read wind velocity, it is best that the flag be at right angles to your view. This makes it easier to see the detailed movement of the tip as it rises and falls with wind velocity changes.

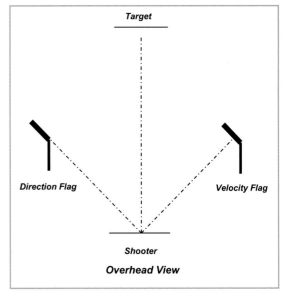

Figure 30. Using two flags—diagram.

Figure 31 and the photographs following in Figures 32 and 33 show flags that would be appropriate for reading wind direction.

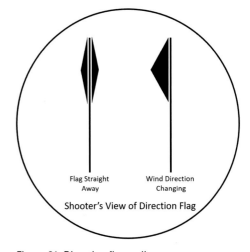

Figure 31. Direction flag—diagram.

Figure 32. Wind toward, wind slightly from the right

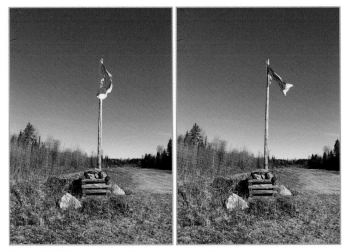

Figure 33. Wind toward, wind slightly from the left.

Figure 34. Wind changing direction (more from the left).

As illustrated in Figures 31–34, to read your "direction flag," you simply find the flag on the range that is blowing directly away or toward you and then use that information to assess the angle of the wind and to monitor any changes in direction.

- Once you have found that flag, continue to monitor it for wind direction.
- When the flag becomes more visible on one side of the pole, you've had a change in wind direction.
- When the flag returns to the "directly away/toward" position, you know you're back to your starting condition.

If you see the flag move to one side of the pole, you know the wind direction has changed. If the flag starts to stay solidly on one side of the pole, start looking for the next flag upwind or downwind, which is now blowing directly toward or away from you. This gives you a new direction flag to monitor. If the wind continues to change direction, keep watching for the pole whose flag is pointing directly toward or away from you.[3]

The "velocity flag" is one that is flying at 90 degrees to your line of sight. This will allow you to see more clearly the flutters and changes as it rises and falls in the wind. You may assess its angle from the pole to estimate the wind velocity, or you may watch its tip rise and fall in relation to a distant landmark, such the horizon, a tree, or a power line, for example.

Figures 35 and 36 show flags that would be appropriate for reading wind velocity.

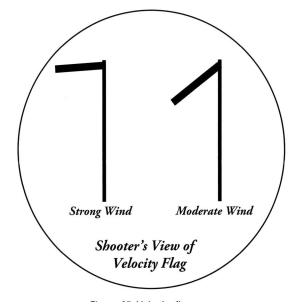

Figure 35. Velocity flag.

Figure 36. Velocity flag at right angles.

Reading Upwind Flags

It is common wisdom that flags that are downwind are telling you about wind that has moved away from you. It is "in the past"; it cannot affect the flight of your bullet and thus is no longer of interest to you, providing you can get better information. And that better information is available on upwind flags. So when you are at the range, try to pick flags that are upwind as these flags are telling you what wind is coming toward you and will be in position to affect the flight of your bullet by the time you launch it.

In Figure 37, the shooter could use the direction flag out in front of his position, but the one behind him is preferable because it is telling him about the wind that is coming to him.

The hardest wind-shoot Linda ever shot required only two flags. As in Figure 37, she had an upwind flag downrange that she could use for speed. She measured the velocity by the height of its tip above the tree line—and it rarely changed. She used an upwind, uprange flag for direction; that flag was right behind her right shoulder. The direction flag changed for almost every shot but had only two values. This was Linda's famous "sandstorm shoot" in the South Africa Palma in 1999, where she shot a possible in conditions so bad that the range staff hadn't even brought the trigger weight to the line—anticipating that no one would get a possible. (A possible means a perfect score. In

target rifle shooting, the trigger weight is checked when a shooter shoots a possible.)

Reading Many Flags

"Since an individual flag has a very small frontal area, the average of several flags should be considered."[4]

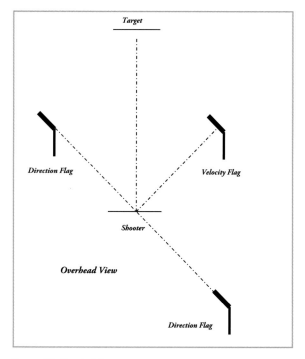

Figure 37. Upwind flags.

The next point to consider is whether one flag for each velocity and direction will be sufficient to monitor the effect of the wind or whether you need to use several flags for velocity and several for direction. The key to deciding how many flags to look at is to understand whether the conditions are uniform (the same throughout your bullet's line of flight) or nonuniform.

- If conditions are uniform, you don't need to watch more than two flags (one for velocity and one for direction).
- If the winds are not uniform, you need to ask yourself, "What's different? Where is it different? And how big is the difference?" What you need to watch depends on the situation, and what you have available to watch depends on the range and your position on it.

Nonuniform Wind Direction

In practical terms, it is rare that you require more than one or possibly two direction flags—and even rarer that you are positioned in a way that enables you to read more than one or two. Usually, you take wind direction from the nearest upwind flag that is blowing directly toward or away from you and that you can reasonably see.

An exception is the situation when you have a swirl going around the range, with the near flags going one way and the far flags going the other. This is quite common on bowl- or saucer-shaped ranges, such as 50-meter smallbore ranges. The best tactic is usually to use the near flags as your primary indicators of the direction, and temper your call with the direction indicated by the far flags.

Nonuniform Wind Velocity

More often, you will need to use more than one flag to appreciate the full velocity of the wind. The first general principle is that if you have a row of flags running the length of your line of fire, and all of them are indicating the same speed, you have a uniform wind condition, and the deflection will be as per the standard wind charts (the maximum for that condition).

For simplicity, in this situation (when conditions are uniform) one flag is all you have to watch. However, if you have nonuniform velocities acting on your bullet, you need to factor in the values appropriately. The near flag is your primary velocity indicator, because it will have the greatest effect on your bullet. Remember the math (chapter 1, "Wind Basics") and realize that it takes a downrange gale to completely counteract an uprange breeze.

If the near flags are still and the far flags are active, then you can estimate the sight correction based on the number of yards that your bullet will travel in the active condition. For example, if the wind picks up at the 500-yard mound and your bullet travels through crosswind for only the remaining

500 yards, you can use your 500-yard velocity chart to estimate your sight setting.

To give you a rough idea of the kind of information you could calculate in detail, Figure 38 estimates the windage corrections required for a 1,000-yard range with two wind conditions, each affecting about half of your bullet's flight. (We provide this chart only to acquaint you with the kinds of wind settings you might need to anticipate. On the range, we recommend that you use the near flags to establish your standard setting, and modify your estimate when the far flags change.)

First 500 yards	Second 500 yards				
	Gentle	Moderate	Fresh	Strong	Very Strong
Gentle	4	5 ¼	6¼	7¾	9½
Moderate	6½	8	9	10½	12¼
Fresh	9	10¼	12	13½	15 ¼
Strong	11 ¾	13	14	16	17¾
Very Strong	14½	15¾	16¾	18 ¼	20

Figure 38. Nonuniform velocity chart.

As Figure 38 shows, if you have a "gentle" wind for both the first 500 yards and the second 500 yards of the bullet's 1,000-yard flight, you will need the standard 4-minute correction. If you have a "gentle" wind for the first 500 yards and a "moderate" wind for the second 500 yards of the bullet's 1,000-yard flight, you will need approximately a 5¼-minute correction. If, on the other hand, you have a "moderate" wind for the first half and a "gentle" wind for the second half, you will need about 6½ minutes.

You can perform exact mathematical assessments based on 100-yard segments, the force of the wind, and the amount of time that your bullet spends in flight (at declining bullet velocities) in each segment.[5] But while this may be an entertaining way to spend a snowbound winter evening, it is unlikely that you'll want to perform all the computations—or even look at a chart—while you're out shooting![6] The fact is that most ranges don't have enough flags to assess wind at any more than two or three points downrange. Moreover, most shooters can only just see major flag changes, much less interpret them at a 100-yard level of detail.

Basic Wind Flag Tactics

In general, your basic tactic should be to eliminate flags that are not relevant (that is, not contributing to improving the accuracy of your wind estimates) and focus on those that are. We have already suggested to you that the essential flags are two near and upwind flags, one for direction and one for speed.

In addition, in nonuniform conditions, use multiple flags to get a true picture of the wind that is acting on your bullet. Use the near flags to estimate your basic wind setting, and use the far flags to modify that setting.

Further, there are some other flags to consider. For example:

- If there is a gap in the land features that permits gusts of wind to act on a flag (and your bullet), you will need to include that flag in your estimate.
- If a flag is buffered by a tree line, it is not going to tell you enough to be helpful (unless the wind switches).
- In a switching wind, you need both upwind and downwind flags, because the direction will be changing.
- On some ranges and in some situations, you need to examine an entire row of flags to understand the total effect of the wind on your bullet's trajectory. If one flag in the row drops, you will have to adjust for it.
- On other ranges, it is important that you visualize the "bowl" mentioned earlier in order to observe the roll and drafts of the wind.
- The most common situation on hard-to-read ranges is that there are conditions that do not show on any of the flags. You may hear an experienced shooter say, "Go with your plot," when something unexpected happens.

This is because, as long as you are firing good shots, your shot fall is your most accurate indicator (it's just after the fact, unfortunately).

And finally, the flag itself has some characteristics of which you need to be aware:

- The fabric and dimensions of the flag affect its behavior, as does the humidity or wetness of the flag.
- In humid conditions, we say the flag is "heavy" or less responsive to the wind. "It should be kept in mind that wet flags will ride at lower levels than dry ones, and these levels will change gradually throughout the drying process."[7]
- A cotton flag is heavier than a nylon one, and the flag with a long, slender tip will dance in the slightest breeze.
- The way the flag is affixed to the pole will also change its appearance, especially in strong wind conditions.

READING MIRAGE

The difficulty of the art of flag reading drives many people to read mirage instead, where the value of wind direction and speed are rolled into one single thing to watch. And since mirage has very little momentum or inertia, it often provides a more accurate picture of wind behavior, because it takes less time to respond to small changes.

However, there is also a significant art to observing and interpreting mirage. Having spent some time on the line with some of Canada's best wind coaches, Linda noticed that some of them could see mirage forming earlier than others, and they were looking for it everywhere. When mirage was light or was just starting to appear—or reappear—the wind coaches would be scanning the edges of everything on the range to try to pick up a little bit of mirage. The coaches with the best scopes typically saw the mirage first, and that's why many national teams use enormous, very powerful scopes for the team matches.

There is also a big debate in mirage reading (as there is in flag reading) about whether you should look at the mirage at the target end (far end) of the range or at the shooter end (near end) of the range. You will recall the "near/far debate" from chapter 2. So you already know that, in purely mathematical terms, the near indicator is best; in fact, about one-third of the distance away from the shooter is generally an effective place to read the wind.

The most common thing we hear from shooters using mirage is this: "I can't see mirage in the middle of the grassy field. I can only see mirage along something with a hard edge, like the target frame." The solution to this situation is to find a hard edge, and then pull the focus of your scope back so that you are focused at an appropriate distance. For example, if you are shooting at 1,000 yards, find the hard edge of the target frame and then pull the focus back until the mound about 300 or 400 yards away from you is in focus. Then look at the hard edge as a background, so you can more clearly see the mirage.

The second difficulty for many target rifle shooters is that by the time the spotting scope is focused correctly for mirage, they can't see the shot indicators well enough to record their shots. (F-Class and precision rifle shooters can use their telescopic sights to view the shot indicators.) We think the best solution is to refocus the scope to spot the shot and then resume the "mirage focus" to watch the wind conditions.

Another challenge that occurs in reading mirage correctly is, as in flag reading, selecting the right point of observation based on the characteristics of the range. The very best example of this that we have ever encountered is at Bisley. One of Great Britain's top shots says he reads the mirage at Stickledown at about the 600-yard mark, just on the forward lip of the big gully in the range floor.

Some of our Canadian champions read the mirage at Connaught by just pulling back the focus of their spotting

scopes to about 30 meters in front of the target. This can work in a big, open field (like the one at Connaught) because the conditions are often uniform for the entire line of fire.

In short, there are two things to consider when you are picking your point of observation for mirage:

- Where is the right point to read flags or mirage in terms of purely mathematical effect on the bullet?
- Where is the right point to read flags or mirage in terms of the peculiarities of a given range and the specific conditions of the day?

The other challenge in reading mirage is that of observing, memorizing, and recalling the exact shape and form of the mirage under specific conditions. This is probably best practiced away from the range—just take your spotting scope out and watch mirage for a while. Start by looking for the things that are easiest to see, for example:

- It is relatively easy to see wind switches in mirage; it is usually clear whether the mirage is "running from the right" or "running from the left."
- Also, the "boil," where the mirage doesn't show a direction but simply stands and streams upward like steam from a pot of boiling water, is very easy to see reliably.

What takes some practice and skill is to read and interpret the differences as the mirage progresses from "running from the right" through "really moving" to "flattened out." However, as with learning to read flags well, the shooter usually needs to recognize only a few conditions to shoot a good match.

We suggest that you learn the five stages of mirage shown below as your basis for learning to read mirage. The stages are as follows:

1. Boiling: 0 to 1 mph
2. Leaning: 1 to 3 mph

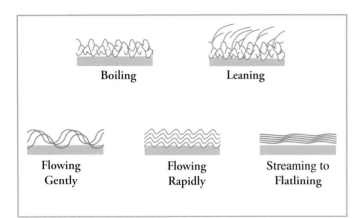

Figure 39. The five stages of mirage.

3. Flowing gently: 4 to 7 mph
4. Flowing rapidly: 8 to 11 mph
5. Streaming to flatlining: 12 mph and more (but not much more)

An important fact about mirage is that it can disappear—it blows off and disappears when the wind reaches about 12 mph (or at least becomes so flat that any further increases in speed are indistinguishable). For this reason, most shooters use mirage in gentle winds, use both flags and mirage in moderate winds, and switch to flags in strong winds. Mirage also disappears when a cloud obscures the sun, and this is another reason that many experienced shooters use both mirage and flags to make their wind calls.

Another critical aspect of reading mirage is appreciating the deflection represented by each of the stages. Figure 40 gives you some examples of the amount of deflection represented by the five stages of mirage at three different distances.

Because mirage is such an excellent tool for gentle (and switching) winds, some shooters may not realize how much wind it can effectively represent. The first time we put this chart together, we were surprised by just how much wind we could read from mirage. At 1,000 yards, we could easily have more than 10 minutes of wind on our sights and still be reading mirage!

Comparison of Flags and Mirage

Figure 41 summarizes and compares the capabilities and characteristics of flags and mirage. Top shooters can use both fluently, and use the best tool at the right time. New shooters first need to learn to use the tools, and with practice will learn when to use flags and when to use mirage.

ENVIRONMENTAL OBSERVATIONS

There are other observation points on the range that can be very useful. One of the commonly used features is the movement of grass, shrubs, and trees; in fact, there are tables available that convert the usual behavior of flora to wind speed in miles per hour. One is included in chapter 1, "Wind Basics."

Mirage		Deflection in Minutes of Angle		
Description & Velocity	Picture	300 yards	600 yards	1000 yards
Boiling; 0–1 mph		0	½	1
Leaning; 1–3 mph		¼	1	2
Flowing gently; 4–7 mph		½	1¾	4
Flowing rapidly 8–11 mph		1¼	3½	8
Streaming to flat-lining; 12 mph +		1¾	5	12

Figure 40. Mirage-deflection chart.

	FLAGS	MIRAGE
Physical Characteristics	• Size and shape • Material and weight • Humidity	• Almost no inertia or momentum • Very sensitive • Usually needs sun
Velocity	• Best at about 4 mph to about 20 mph	• Excellent in gentle winds • Flatlines at about 12 mph
Direction	• Shows wind speed and direction separately	• Shows speed and direction in one value • Excellent at showing wind switches from 11 to 1 o'clock
Upwind-Downwind	• Best to read upwind flags (wind coming to you)	• Most shooters view mirage on their own firing point
Real estate	• Each flag shows a small sample of the total situation, so combine the values of several flag readings	• Mirage provides a consolidated view of a cone of air, but doesn't sample the higher air layers required for long range
Near or far	• Give more weight to value of near flags than far flags	• Often easiest to read at target end, best to read about ⅓ downrange of the shooter
First sighter or subsequent shots	• Good for initial wind value estimate	• Good for seeing changes
Equipment required	• Easy to discern with unaided eye	• Usually requires scoping, the best scope is best

Figure 41. Comparative summary of flags and mirage.

Linda's medal-winning smallbore shoot in the 1995 Cuba World Cup was the result of noticing that a small-leafed ground cover right in front of the firing line was the only indicator that warned of an 8-ring wind. In international smallbore, if the team is big enough, a spotter is assigned to the shooter during the match. The spotter's role is to record the flag position and the shot fall.

Following the match, Linda's spotter rushed up to her, very excited. "What were you doing? You had one of the best shoots out there, but I couldn't see what you were doing! The flags would change, and you didn't touch your sights and still you got a ten! Were you aiming off?"

The truth was that the flags were not good indicators of true conditions on that day. The true indicator was this little ground cover: when the wind picked up enough to rustle the leaves, it was a 9-ring wind; when it picked up enough to start to turn the leaves over, it was an 8-ring wind. It took Linda a few lost points to make these discoveries, but many shooters never found a good indicator that day and consequently lost many more points.

Your neighbors' shots are another useful wind-reading tool. Neighboring shots, particularly on targets upwind to yours, can provide good information about what is happening. Once your own group is well centered, look at where the average shot placement is on the targets upwind of your own target. If everyone continues to be well centered, continue with your own estimation of the wind. But if there are suddenly a number of shots out to one side, look for a subtle condition change that others may have missed.

The comments of your neighbors may also give you a reason to take a look around and make sure you haven't missed a change in conditions. We have often been lulled into a false sense of security by a series of successful shots with a single sight setting and probably would have carried on blissfully if we had not overheard a neighbor say, "Oh, darn!"

Dust kicked up by neighboring shots as they strike the butts can provide information. Watch the drifting dust to see how quickly it moves and in what direction. We have often found this very helpful in service rifle shooting, where there are often few if any flags and where the courses of fire (snaps, rapids, or fire and movement) don't lend themselves to using a spotting scope to observe mirage. In addition, there may be bits of debris in the air, dandelion or other plant seed parasols, or pieces of paper. If there is long grass, it will lean in the wind. On some occasions, you will be able to watch the smoke from adjacent black powder shooters. These are not necessarily the best wind indicators, but on some ranges they may be your only indicators.

On one occasion, at a World Cup in Mexico City, the best wind indicator on the smallbore range was the dust kicked up in the butts by the impact of the bullets. There was almost no wind at the shooter end of the range, and the flags were often conflicting and often vertical. Since the range was wide open, the shooters could see everyone else's shot impact. The dust would respond to the shots, and signal the wind's behavior. Sometimes the dust would puff straight up, hang in the air, and then fall back onto the butts. With a little wind, it would puff straight up at first and then drift sideways. With a little more wind, it would rise up diagonally and drift for some distance at that angle. With a fairly good wind, it would rise up diagonally and then go horizontal before disappearing. Each of these behaviors indicated a different wind condition and a different sight setting. While this is not a particularly conventional way to read the wind, when it is the only way, it is the best way!

And, finally, if you're observing conditions before you go up to shoot, shooters coming off the line are often a good source of information, especially if you have a conversation starter such as, "I saw the wind fishtail and you went from bull to bull—how did you do that?"

WIND-READING DEVICES

Wind-reading devices are very helpful as training aids. It is usually against the rules to use such devices on the firing point while shooting a match, but they provide useful information before you go up to shoot. These devices come in two common forms: a small handheld wind meter and a complete weather station with an anemometer (see Figures 42 and 43).[8]

They will very accurately read the wind speed, and, knowing this, you can relate it to the flags. You will soon begin to recognize correct wind speeds from the flags and, of course, this *is* information you can use on the firing point.

When you visit a foreign range, you cannot be certain that the flags are the same as the ones on your home range. As

Figure 42. Handheld wind meter.

noted earlier, their fabric and size will affect how sensitive they are to the wind. Having a wind meter will help you recalibrate your senses to deal with unfamiliar flags. And if the humidity is significantly higher or lower than usual (caused by rain, heavy dew, or changes in relative humidity), a wind meter can help you understand what effect these conditions are having on the flags.

Estimating wind speed is more difficult than determining wind direction. A wind meter can help you learn to judge the wind—even by feel—more accurately. You can practice anytime you are outdoors.

We worked with one special police force whose members would, every time they jumped out of their truck, make an immediate estimate (by feel) of the wind velocity and then follow it up with a reading on their wind meter. We thought this was such a good idea that we started doing it too. We were pleasantly surprised just how quickly our ability to estimate wind velocity by feel improved and just how accurate it became.

Figure 43. Weather station in use on a police course.

We use the complete weather station when we are teaching our police sniper and competition wind-reading courses, so that the students can accurately relate all the indicators that are used in the field to what is really happening.

Interpreting Your Observations

Once you have learned to observe wind indicators carefully and in accurate detail, you need to be able to convert your observations into sight settings (or into amounts to aim off). There are several sources of this information, including:

• The classic Wind Calculator by Alfred J. Parker Ltd., a paper pinwheel that exposes the sight settings for various ranges by means of rotating the paper wheel past a cutout window. It is specifically for the NATO 7.62mm cartridge.

• Wind flag diagrams, which show the sight settings for various wind velocities and angles, given the distance. These are usually based on data for the NATO 7.62mm cartridge, and the flag diagrams are based on Bisley (heavy) flags. They are often included on commercially available plotting diagrams.

• Ballistics software programs, which convert your specific environmental and load characteristics into deflection (usually in inches or centimeters, which then must be converted into minutes or milrads).[9] This information can then be built into your own charts or flag diagrams. The software programs normally include a wide range of cartridges, and you can vary the information to exactly represent your own handloads.

In this book, we have used data from all these sources for our examples. The Tools Appendix includes a full set of our wind charts and diagrams.

Using Wind Charts

Charts can be very useful to get a feeling for what wind to start with and to give you an idea of what the bookends might be before you fire your first shot. (Once you have established this basic information from the charts, then you fire your first shot and start using data from your shot indication. During a course of fire, you would refer back to charts only if there were a major change outside the bookends you had previously identified.)

There are lots of different kinds of charts. Look at them all and find one that you can understand easily. It should be handy and easy to keep with you so that it will be there when you need it. It should be designed so that it is easy to control with one hand on a windy firing point.

Most commercially available wind charts come in a series of pages, which can be a little awkward to use in competition. The challenge is to provide enough information yet keep the right information easy to find.

MilCun Police Sniper Charts

The following charts (Figures 44 and 45) are the ones that we use and teach on our police sniper courses. We simply print the charts on a size that fits in our shooting book (half a standard letter-size page) and then laminate it to protect it from abuse and precipitation.

SPEED	Kph	5	10	15	20	25	30	35	40	45	50
DIRECTION	Mph	3	6	9	12	15	18	22	25	28	31
Degrees	O'clock										
0	12:00, 6:00	0	0	0	0	0	0	0	0	0	0
10		1	1	2	2	3	3	4	4	5	5
15	11:30, 12:30, 5:30, 6:30	1	2	2	3	4	5	6	6	7	8
20		1	2	3	4	5	6	8	9	10	11
30	11:00, 1:00, 5:00, 7:00	2	3	5	6	8	9	11	13	14	16
40		2	4	6	8	10	12	14	16	18	20
45	10:30, 1:30, 4:30, 7:30	2	4	7	9	11	13	16	18	20	22
50		2	5	7	10	12	14	17	19	21	24
60	10:00, 2:00, 4:00, 8:00	3	5	8	11	13	16	19	22	24	27
70		3	6	9	12	15	17	21	24	26	29
75	2:30, 3:30, 8:30, 9:30	3	6	9	12	15	18	21	24	27	30
80		3	6	9	12	15	18	22	25	28	31
90	3:00, 9:00	3	6	9	12	15	18	22	25	28	31

Figure 44. Wind value conversion chart.

The primary advantage of these charts is that you need only two charts for all distances and conditions. (Another chart is provided in the Tools Appendix to provide metric distances, as well as a number of charts for several popular calibers.)

The MilCun charts are easy to use, following these three steps:

1. The first step to using any chart is the same, no matter the chart. You must first make your best assessment of the wind direction and speed. For example, let's say that the wind is blowing from 11 o'clock at about 15 kph (9 mph).

2. You then apply this information to the wind value conversion chart shown in Figure 44.

   a. First you select the row that best represents the direction the wind is coming from. In our example, you would find the row labeled 30 degrees or 11 o'clock.

   b. Then you read across that row to the column that represents the velocity of the wind. In our example, you would find the column labeled 15 kph or 9 mph.

   The number in that square (intersection of direction and speed) is a "wind value" number, which is used in the next step. In our example, the square that this row and column intersect contains a value of 5. (The wind value number basically converts all readings to a constant, which happens to be 90 degrees.)

3. Once you have your wind value number, you move to the windage chart (Figure 45—this chart is for .308 Match, 155-grain Sierra bullet with a muzzle velocity of 3,100 fps). Once you find the appropriate wind value, you simply move across the row to the column for the distance from which you are shooting. The number in the box is the sight setting in minutes of angle.

To complete our example, we would find the number 5 in the Wind Value column of the windage chart and then move across that row to find the sight settings for various distances. If we were shooting at a distance of 600 yards, we would expect to need 2 minutes of wind on our sight.

Wind Flag Diagrams

For shooters who are less chart oriented and more picture oriented, a different style of wind chart may be more useful. Linda prefers the wind flag diagrams shown in Figure 46. The main disadvantages are that you need one diagram for each distance and that the level of precision is somewhat lower than with the charts previously discussed. The primary advantage of the Wind Flag Diagram is that a change in wind condition can easily and quickly be assessed and assigned a sight setting.

Windage Chart for 155-grain .308 Match—Yards
155-gr Sierra MK; MV 3100 fps; BC .455; Temp 77°F; Elev 600 ft

Wind Value	Range in Yards									
	100	200	300	400	500	600	700	800	900	1000
1	.1	.1	.2	.3	.3	.4	.5	.6	.7	.9
2	.1	.3	.4	.5	.7	.9	1.0	1.2	1.5	1.7
3	.2	.4	.6	.8	1.0	1.3	1.6	1.9	2.2	2.5
4	.2	.5	.8	1.0	1.4	1.7	2.1	2.5	2.9	3.4
5	.3	.6	1.0	1.3	1.7	2.1	2.6	3.1	3.6	4.2
6	.4	.7	1.1	1.6	2.0	2.6	3.1	3.7	4.4	5.1
7	.4	.9	1.3	1.8	2.4	3.0	3.6	4.3	5.1	5.9
8	.5	1.0	1.5	2.1	2.7	3.4	4.1	4.9	5.8	6.8
9	.5	1.1	1.7	2.4	3.1	3.8	4.6	5.5	6.5	7.6
10	.6	1.2	1.9	2.6	3.4	4.3	5.2	6.2	7.3	8.5
11	.7	1.3	2.1	2.9	3.7	4.7	5.7	6.8	8.0	9.3
12	.7	1.5	2.3	3.1	4.1	5.5	6.2	7.4	8.7	10.2
13	.8	1.6	2.5	3.4	4.4	5.5	6.7	8.0	9.4	11.0
14	.8	1.7	2.7	3.7	4.8	5.9	7.2	8.6	10.2	11.8
15	.9	1.8	2.8	3.9	5.1	6.4	7.7	9.2	10.9	12.7
16	.9	2.0	3.0	4.2	5.4	6.8	8.3	9.9	11.6	13.5
17	1.0	2.1	3.2	4.5	5.8	7.2	8.8	10.5	12.3	14.4
18	1.1	2.2	3.4	4.7	6.1	7.6	9.3	11.1	13.1	15.2
19	1.1	2.3	3.6	5.0	6.5	8.1	9.8	11.7	13.8	16.1
20	1.2	2.4	3.8	5.2	6.8	8.5	10.3	12.3	14.5	16.9
21	1.2	2.6	4.0	5.5	7.1	8.9	10.8	12.9	15.3	17.8
22	1.3	2.7	4.2	5.8	7.5	9.3	11.4	13.6	16.0	18.6
23	1.4	2.8	4.4	6.0	7.8	9.8	11.9	14.2	16.7	19.5
24	1.4	2.9	4.5	6.3	8.2	10.2	12.4	14.8	17.4	20.3
25	1.5	3.1	4.7	6.5	8.5	10.6	12.9	15.4	18.2	21.2
26	1.5	3.2	4.9	6.8	8.8	11.0	13.4	16.0	18.9	22.0
27	1.6	3.3	5.1	7.1	9.2	11.5	13.9	16.6	19.6	22.8
28	1.7	3.4	5.3	7.3	9.5	11.9	14.5	17.3	20.3	23.7
29	1.7	3.5	5.5	7.6	9.9	12.3	15.0	17.9	21.1	24.5
30	1.8	3.7	5.7	7.9	10.2	12.8	15.5	18.5	21.8	25.4
31	1.8	3.8	5.9	8.1	10.6	13.2	16.0	19.1	22.5	26.2

Figure 45. Windage chart for .308 Match (155 grain).

The example in Figure 46 is a wind flag diagram for 1,000 yards.[10]

1. First you pick the flag symbol (or wind-speed range) that most closely represents the wind velocity.
2. Then you follow the horizontal line from that flag across to a diagonal line. The diagonal lines represent the direction of the wind. The first one represents a 1 o'clock wind, the second one represents a 2 o'clock wind, and the third one represents a 3 o'clock wind.
3. From that intersection (of the horizontal velocity line and the diagonal direction line), go straight up to the top and read the windage sight setting in minutes of angle.

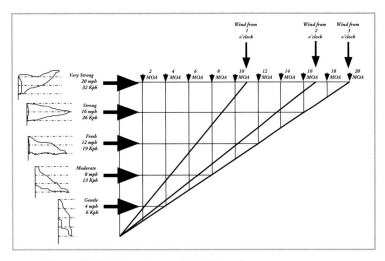

Figure 46. Wind flag diagram for 1,000 yards.

For example, if we think that the wind is "fresh" and from 3 o'clock, we can follow the "fresh" horizontal line across until it meets the 3 o'clock line at the extreme right-hand side. Then we follow the vertical line at that intersection up and read the number of minutes of correction at top of the chart. In our example, the correction would be 12 minutes.

A different diagram is required for each distance that you shoot. A set of these diagrams (for standard target rifle competition distances) is provided in the Tools Appendix.

As previously mentioned, you need to calibrate the wind flags that are available at your range so that you know what velocity each one represents. Then you need to calibrate the wind flag diagram so that the sight correction (in minutes of angle) accurately represents your caliber and load. The diagram shown above represents the standard 7.62 NATO round commonly issued by the military in NATO countries. If you are using a more efficient round (such as 6mm BR or 6.5mm-284), you will need to adapt the diagram to reflect the appropriate sight adjustments.

RECORDING METHODS AND TOOLS

Using Replicas
Many shooters in many different disciplines use replicas of

the target to keep track of their shot placement. Electronic targets do this for you automatically, showing the current shot, as well as any number of past shots you wish to see. In long-range shooting, where you are shown the location of each shot fall one at a time, it is very hard to recall more than just a couple of past shots, even when you are shooting single string. If you are shooting in pairs and threesomes (where you shoot in turn with one or two other shooters), it is hard to remember more than one in a row of your own shots. To overcome this, most shooters jot something down on a picture of the target in their record books. For example, the target replica shown in Figure 47 would be kept in the shooter's diary book and marked with the shots as they were indicated during the course of fire.

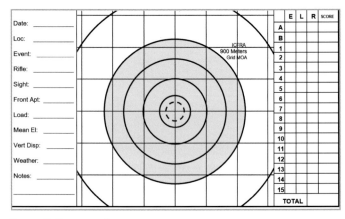

Figure 47. Target replica.

For those who aim off, two replicas are required. One replica is used to record the aim point for the shot, and the other is used to record the shot fall. For example, on the diary page shown in Figure 48, the shooter would record shot fall on the larger replica and would record the point of aim on the mini-replica. Some "aim off-ers" use only one replica, and record the aim points in one color of pen and the shot fall in another.

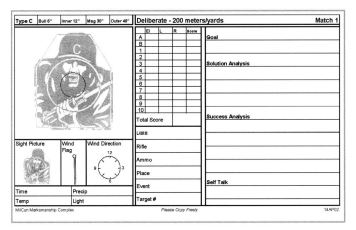

Figure 48. Target replica with mini-replica.

This simple method falls short when more than one sight setting is used during the course of the match. It is very hard to indicate (or to remember without indicating) what setting was used for which shots. Thus must surely have arisen the fine "auld British" tradition of graphing.

Graphing

When shooting in twos or threes, it is important to keep track of the shots that you have fired and the sight settings used. Ideally, you want to be able to compare shots within the context of the sight setting used to fire each one. That way, you can use all the information you have gathered on a common basis to help you keep your group centered and to make well-informed wind decisions.

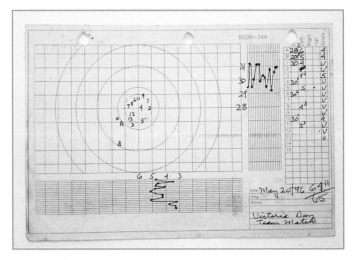

Figure 49. Graphing.

Graphing is an old and time-honored way of doing this, as you can see in Figure 49. With each shot fired, you record the elevation and windage used on your sight, and you record the shot placement on a scale replica of the target. To the side and below the replica, you have two separate graphs. One graph represents what the elevation should have been set at to produce a centered shot for elevation; the other represents what the windage should have been set at to produce a centered shot for windage.

By analyzing the elevation graph, the shooter can see what his mean elevation setting should have been and can anticipate that he might need this setting for his next shots. By analyzing the wind graph, the shooter can see what settings would have been required to center his shots for wind. If he was attentive to the conditions that were present when those shots were fired, he can anticipate what windage setting he will need when they arise again.

This method is widely used in the Commonwealth countries, so we were surprised when one of Britain's top shooters said that he didn't believe in it. His point was that shooters spend far too much time recording and analyzing what is already past (and therefore no longer important) and far too little time actually watching the conditions.[11]

We personally believe that traditional graphing has been surpassed in effectiveness by the Plot-o-Matic (EZ-Graf).

The Plot-o-Matic (EZ-Graf)

A simpler and faster way of recording and analyzing the same information is an ingenious device invented by George Chase of New Brunswick, Canada, called a Plot-o-Matic (EZ-Graf).[12]

As shown in Figure 50, a target replica is placed under a sheet of clear plastic, such as Plexiglas or Lexan. The plastic sheet is held in a frame so that it moves vertically (to represent elevation) and horizontally (to represent windage). The

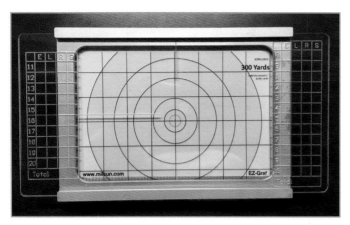

Figure 50. The plot-o-matic (EZ-Graf).

Figure 51. Group forming on the plot-o-matic (EZ-Graf).

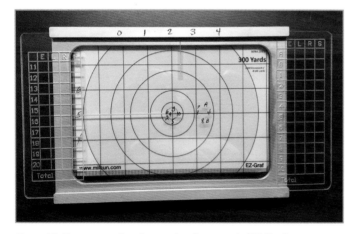

Figure 52. Two groups forming on the plot-o-matic (EZ-Graf).

for the current practice or match. There is an index line scribed in the Plexiglas, and the shooter moves the Plexiglas so that each shot can be plotted within the context of the sight setting used. Once the shot is plotted, the shooter can move the Plexiglas to center the shot over the target replica. Then the shooter uses the index line to read the correct sight setting off the horizontal and vertical scales.

In Figure 51, a small group is forming with a sight setting of 5 minutes of elevation and 1 minute of right wind.

The Plot-o-Matic (EZ-Graf) results in a very fast and very visual appreciation of the correct sight setting, as you can see in the photo. This helps the shooter center the group both vertically and horizontally, because he can see a picture of the group forming (and he doesn't have to do the math required for graphing or read a graph to apply the information it represents).

Figure 52 shows two groups forming. With the Plot-o-Matic (EZ-Graf), it is particularly easy to see two or more wind conditions developing (because two distinct groups form as the shooter records shot fall, regardless of whether he called the wind correctly for each shot). In Figure 52, you can see that there are two distinct wind conditions, shown by the two groups. One of the wind conditions needs 1 minute of right wind to center it, and the other group needs about 2¼ minutes right to center it.[13]

By combining recording and analyzing into a single step, the Plot-o-Matic (EZ-Graf) provides a much more visual picture of wind conditions and group formation than any other method we have found. (For more information about, and suppliers of, the Plot-o-Matic [EZ-Graf], see Appendix B, Resources.)

The Plot-o-Matic (EZ-Graf) can also be used by those who aim off to show the correct aim point required to produce a center shot. The shooter simply puts the index mark at the aim point and plots the shot fall. By moving the shot to the

target replica has horizontal and vertical scales in minutes of angle to represent sight settings.

The shooter marks the Plot-o-Matic (EZ-Graf) with numbers to represent the sight settings he expects to use center of the replica, the Plot-o-Matic (EZ-Graf) index mark will fall on the desired aim point to correct for that shot.

Analyzing Graphs and Plots

No matter which device you use, there are several things that you should be looking for in your analysis.

Regardless of wind conditions, you should use your plotting (or graphing) information to center your group, both elevation-wise and wind-wise. The importance of centering your group cannot be overemphasized.[14] What you're trying to do is give your bullet maximum opportunity to hit the bull's-eye, and to do this you need to give it maximum real estate.

For every shot fired, the shooter needs to imagine that it is part of a group. The first sighter that is fired could represent the left of the group, the right of the group, the top of the group, the bottom of the group, or any point within the group. The second sighter helps to establish where the group is going to form, but, statistically, it is the third shot that is most likely to complete the correct picture.

Regardless of the number of individual shots fired, the shooter must always be analyzing the whole group (assuming that the group is fired under similar conditions).

As shown in Figure 53, if you have a 1¼-minute group (the best target rifle shooters in the world look to have 1¼ vertical dispersion!) and the average bull's-eye is 2 minutes in diameter (they vary by type of match, but most of the target rifle bull's-eyes are about 2 minutes), then you have only ¾ of a minute (⅜ on each side of center) before your shots are starting to creep out of the bull.[15] If you can call the wind within ½ minute (and the best in the world can do this only at short ranges!), you still run odds of having one slip out.

In short, given a world-class grouping capability (rifle, ammunition, and shooter's hold), you also need to be a top-notch wind reader—and have your group perfectly centered

in the bull—to keep all your shots in (and even so, they may slip out the edges, at 3 o'clock or 9 o'clock, if you miss that ½-minute wind call).[16]

Figure 54. Grouping high in the bull.

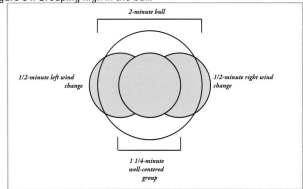

Figure 53. The well-centered group.

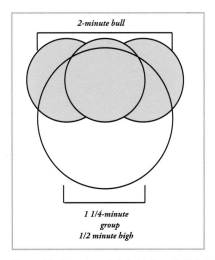

Figure 55. Grouping slightly high and slightly left.

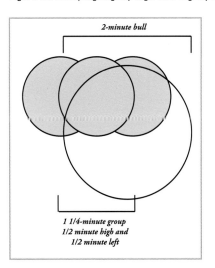

47

If your group is a little high in the bull, as shown in Figure 54, you are running even more risky odds. Notice that as your group rises in the bull, you have less horizontal space. Many shooters have commented that they lose their shots out on the "corners" on the bull and that they wish the bull's-eye were square. They would be better off wishing that they had centered the group so that they had maximum real estate available for their shots.

To emphasize this point one final time, take a look at the groups in Figure 55. These groups represent an outstanding shooter whose sight setting is ½ minute high and ½ minute left. The wind conditions are very slight, requiring only ½-minute corrections either side of center. All these small errors result in the possibility that the shooter will put only half his well-fired shots in the bull.

It cannot be overemphasized that, before you can become a good wind shooter, you must be able to recognize your grouping capability, and you must be able to center your group.

YOUR WIND-READING TOOLBOX

There are different approaches to the game of wind calling. The general purpose of most techniques and tactics is to reduce the complexity of making the call while improving the odds that the call is accurate enough to give you the best possible score for the conditions.

- Sometimes, there are conservative approaches that will keep you in the bull and riskier ones that, if you predict the wind exactly, will keep you in the V-bull.
- The size of the bull may be a factor if the wind is tricky but not easy to predict.
- Occasionally, you may decide that a "good shoot" under the conditions would be to get all your shots in the black, so you choose your tactics to accomplish that and leave the V-chasing to a day with better conditions.

If you pay attention to what technique you are using, you can start to collect a variety of tools for your wind-reading toolbox; then you can choose, from a well-practiced selection, the best tool for the day, the match, or the shot.

When you decide that you are going to focus on developing your wind-reading skills, you should start with just one or at most two techniques and practice them until you become really good at them. And you should eventually learn to use as many techniques as possible, because each day—and each range—may bring the need for a different one.

Being able to use more than one technique at a time can help confirm your observations. More than one technique is also helpful to ensure that at least one will still be readable, though others may falter (e.g., mirage disappears, but flags are still readable).

You should collect tactics and techniques in your wind-reading toolbox, so you can pull out the right tool for the situation you are in. We have grouped our tactics and techniques into three categories:

1. Pre-match preparation
2. Game plan
3. Shot-by-shot tactics

PRE-MATCH PREPARATION

Before the match, often months or even years before the match, you start preparing. You may not think of this period as "match preparation," but it surely is. You are building your basic skills, practicing your fundamental techniques, and gathering your set of tools and tactics.

Firing a Perfect Shot

In competition, there is nothing so completely empowering—and so completely necessary—as knowing that you can fire a perfect shot on demand.

The first time Linda became fully aware of this empowerment was at the Ontario Provincial Championships in 1999. At that point, she had been a successful shooter for almost 15 years, yet she had not tasted the power of knowing that her performance could be perfect. As she wrote in "Snatch the Pebble":

> The first day of the matches dawned sweet and soft, my favorite kind of Canadian summer day. I felt confident that I *knew* exactly what I needed to do to shoot a perfect shot, to read the wind and set my sights and fire a perfect shot. I felt confident that I *could do* what I needed to do to shoot a perfect shot and then another and then another.
>
> I honestly don't remember much of the second day. Just shooting shot after perfect shot, as perfect as I could make them.[17]

Knowing Your System's Grouping Capabilities

You, your rifle, and your ammunition combine to produce the system that performs together to shoot the smallest possible groups at every range. Knowing what your system can do is a critical part of being able to determine an effective game plan for a match and to separate wind-caused displacements from group size.

When you are determining your game plan for a match, you need to understand what the total capability of your system is. If your capability is a 1-minute group, you can choose and use game plans that would not be appropriate if your group size was 2 minutes.

During the match when you place a shot just inside the bull line at 3 o'clock, you need to be able to assess whether that shot is part of your system's group or whether your group needs to be centered.

Understanding Long-Range Bullet Drift

As mentioned earlier, because the bullet spins as it moves through the air, it is subject to a slight gyroscopic effect. The standard target rifle with clockwise rifling imparts a clockwise spin on the bullet, and this spin gradually moves the bullet to the right as it flies forward. Over a distance of 1,000 yards, the total effect is about 1 minute.

The only time it is really noticeable is when you are dealing with either a headwind or a tailwind. When the flags drop to zero and the mirage is boiling, you might be tempted to set your sight on zero and fire this relatively easy shot—and then wonder why it is a nipper on the right side. Or, when you are faced with a wind that switches on each side of 12 o'clock, it can be confusing to set 1 minute left on the sight for a boil and 0 for a slight right wind. (During other wind conditions, with the wind strongly from one side or another, the effect tends to disappear within our wind estimate.)

To address this problem, some shooters use two rear sights, one for short range and one for long range. Each is carefully zeroed for wind at the appropriate range, so that true zero is accurately set on the sight. If you use a Plot-o-Matic (EZ-Graf), it is relatively simple to mark the true zero on the frame so that you can deal with a switching wind (it crosses from right to left wind, at 1 minute left instead of 0).

If you get the chance to test this out on a 1,000-yard range under zero-wind conditions, do so and see what kind of drift you are getting. Then record the difference on your charts and graphs so that you will allow for this the next time you are shooting at long range.

Having a Wind-Training Plan

The best advice on wind training is the simplest, and it comes from Canada's Des Burke: "Practice in difficult conditions."[18] A fair-weather shooter is only ever going to be a fair-weather winner.

You can learn to fire perfect shots in good conditions, but you need bad conditions to learn to read the wind. When you get an opportunity to shoot hard winds, make sure you have a plan.

Figure out what you're trying to learn from this training opportunity; have a game plan; use it; and, after you're done, assess what you learned.

Doing a Range "Recce" from Afar[19]

Before you go to a new range, do your homework. Try to find out as much as you can before you get there. It's certainly easier to do this today than ever before. You can find shooters who have visited the range and talk to them in person, by phone, or by email. Many shooters are now using digital cameras and can easily send you a photo of the range electronically. The Internet can help you "visit" other countries, and some ranges and rifle associations have Web sites that can help you visualize the range before you get there.

Make creative use of the Internet. Research the range property itself through the shooting associations that host matches there, and the local topography through government organizations or map sellers. Get a description of seasonal conditions (including predominant wind patterns) through the local weather office. Email other shooters to ask questions and get advice.

Here's the kind of information you can seek out:

- What does the range look like? What vegetation does it have? What is its topography?
- Can you get any pictures? Can you get a satellite picture?
- What flags are available? Where are they? How tall are the flagpoles? What material are the flags made of? What size are they?
- What are the daily patterns of the wind for the time of year that you will be there?
- What are the keys to understanding the airflow on the range?
- What lessons have others learned while shooting on that range? Can you talk to anyone who has done wind coaching there?

Keep a record of everything you learn in your shooting diary, and when you get on site start adding the details.

GAME PLAN

Game plan tactics and techniques are focused around the efforts you make for a specific event. The event could be a single match as short as a few shots or may include several matches over several days or weeks. The point is that you will want an approach for the whole event, as well as for each of the individual shooting opportunities. From a wind-reading perspective, the tactics you choose for the whole event usually focus on the range itself, while the tactics you choose for the individual shooting opportunity focus on the specific conditions you anticipate having on that day and at that time of day.

Doing a Range Recce on Site

"If the wind is from the front . . . it gets to you *after* it covers the range. Therefore, try to select at least one indicator way down the range, and preferably on the same side of the range as the wind is coming from. . . . If the wind is from the rear . . . look for the nearest indicator you can find to your shooting position, especially one on the same side as the wind is coming from."[20]

When you arrive at the range for the match, take a look around. Confirm that what you learned from your "range recce from afar" is accurate or that what you already knew about the range from previous visits hasn't changed.

On some particular ranges, the effects of ground contours need to be taken into account; for example, Stickledown range at Bisley has a significant gully and a break in the tree line at about midrange, producing a wind effect that is different from what you might read at any other point in the length of the range. Drawing a sketch of the range, including the topography, such natural features as trees, and the positions of flagpoles, is a useful tool to help your accurate observation of the range, and a useful aide-mémoire when you return to the same range.

While you are drawing your sketch of the range, you can try to visualize it like a big swimming pool, with air currents in three dimensions. This will help you identify the "roll" of air as it sweeps over and around the landforms. Stickledown has high ground on the right side, dropping off to the left. Because of this slope, the wind's effect will be different coming from one side compared to the other. Think about the effect of the wind from various directions.

If your range reconnaissance has been thorough, you may have visited the local weather office and gotten information that can be used to construct a rose of winds. Following is an example of the rose of winds for the MilCun Marksmanship Complex range in Ontario, Canada. It shows that for the summer months:

- The primary wind condition is a wind from the west to west-northwest, varying from about 7 to 17 kph (about 4 to 10 mph).
- The secondary wind condition is a wind from the south-southeast, varying from about 5 to 15 kph (about 3 to 9 mph).
- Most other wind directions are under 5 kph (about 3 mph).

While this does not give you the conditions for the day or for your match, it certainly tells you that average conditions at this location are going to be relatively mild. It also tells you what the "normal" dominant winds are, which can be useful

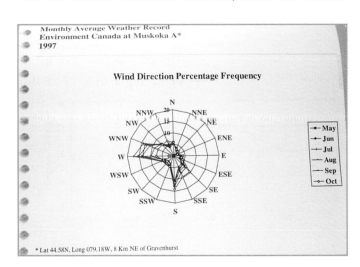

Figure 56. Rose of winds.

in picking your indicators. And it forewarns you that any other conditions you may see probably indicate a storm, an inversion, or some other type of unstable air.

Choosing Your Wind Indicators

Which wind indicators are best to use will change according to conditions. Your research will have given you some idea of what the dominant condition is at the range. But there is no substitute for a firsthand study of what is going on at the range. Spend as much time as you can doping out the conditions, looking for the dominant condition in the morning, at midday, and in the afternoon. Look also for the secondary conditions at these times, and notice what the pattern is when the wind is changing from one condition to another. For example, if you are at an inland range, that alternate condition may be about 90 degrees from the dominant condition; but if you are at a coastal range, it could be 180 degrees from the dominant condition (due to the land breeze-sea breeze effect).

Draw a diagram of the range, showing the firing mounds and the key land features. The land features (e.g., tree lines, ridges, gullies, slopes, and waterways) affect the flow of air. Draw in the positions of the flagpoles. Show the dominant condition with a heavy arrow, and show the secondary condition with a thinner arrow.

Picture the wind blowing from the dominant direction, and determine which indicators will tell you the best story. Look at what's available for wind indicators when you are on the left side of the range, at both short and long range. Then look at it from the point of view of the right-side firing points, at both short and long range.

Then picture the wind blowing from the alternate condition, and determine which indicators will give you the most accurate information. Again, think in terms of being given a firing point on the left (short and long ranges) and on the right (short and long ranges).

Often, when you work through a practical example like this one, you find that there are not very many candidate flags, and you will have to use the best of what's available. Sometimes, though, on a big, open range, such as De Wet Range in South Africa, you'll have a choice of flags. Keeping in mind our discussion earlier in this chapter on flag reading, and the use of two or more flags, choose the ones that will give you the best information.

Some Final Thoughts on Which Flags to Use

We believe that it is theoretically better to have a sense of the complete action of the wind during the bullet's entire trajectory. However, in practical terms, it is rare that there are enough flags to make that assessment. And even if there were, doing the math is going to take longer than the condition would last!

So from a very practical point of view, what we do is assess the wind based on the near flags and modify our assessment based on the activity of the far flags. For example:

- If all the flags are indicating a "strong" wind from 3 o'clock (about 16 mph, or 25 kph), we expect a 16-minute sight correction.
- If the near flags indicate a strong wind and the far flags are showing "very strong" (about 20 mph, or 32 kph), we expect to add a little, perhaps 1 to 2 minutes, to our 16-minute setting, for a total of 17 to 18 minutes.
- If the near flags indicate a "strong" wind and the far flags are showing only "fresh," we expect to subtract a little, perhaps 1 to 2 minutes, from our 16-minute setting, for a total of 14 to 15 minutes.

And, finally, as we all know from our own shooting experience, the flag we wish we had is not always there. While in theory we might prefer a near flag (and an upwind near flag at that), in practical terms we often must make do with what we've got. In those cases, we need to spend a little time during our on-site range recce figuring out what wind conditions could occur that would not show on our flags

and what actions we could take to protect ourselves from a nasty surprise.

Using Mirage

Sometimes the right answer is in the mirage. Especially in light winds, when the flags are not particularly responsive, and when light winds are switching, mirage can be your best indicator. And mirage can often give you more accurate information at short ranges, where there are not many flags available and those that are available are flying well above the trajectory of your bullet.

On the range, we often hear a wide variety of opinions about where the mirage should be read. Many shooters read the mirage from the edge of the target board or the number board, even though the bullet's flight to the target will not pass through this air. One of Canada's top shooters told us that he tries to pick up ground mirage a couple of hundred yards in front of his firing position. Many shooters pull the spotting scope focus back from the target (probably less than a hundred yards) because it is convenient and they can still see the target well enough to spot their shots.

If you "cruise" the range floor with your scope, you will start to get a feel for where you can read mirage on the range. And reading it near your firing point, as well as downrange, may well pay off. As Des Burke noted, "There may be times when in light winds a slight left mirage shows at the target end and a right wind at the firing end. These are usually light winds, and a simple compromise between the two, favoring the firing mound end wind value, is necessary."[21]

What Others Say About Mirage

From *Target Rifle Shooting* by E.G.B. Reynolds and Robin Fulton:

Reynolds and Fulton emphasize that the ability to read mirage accurately can be developed only through practice. Becoming sensitive to the details takes time in the scope, and translating what you see to a wind value (and a sight setting) takes experience. They advocate what most long-range shooters agree about: the spotting scope should be focused about one-third the distance from the shooter to the target. They also maintain that mirage is most useful when the winds are gentle, which is when there is very little movement in the flags. (In fact, if mirage is not present, the shooter will often look at such details of the flag as on which side of the pole it is resting.) Mirage continues to be useful through light winds, especially in fishtailing winds, where its quick response to change is an asset. At 7 or 8 miles per hour, mirage starts to be difficult to read, and it is better to rely on the flags.

From *Canadian Bisley Shooting* by Desmond T. Burke:

"The mirage should be a superior indicator since one can focus on a fairly long sector . . . at the target end of the range without blurring the target too much for spotting. This zone can be increased by using a lower power scope . . . The focus should not be changed incessantly during a shoot; otherwise the shooter will alter the appearance of the mirage and its animation sufficiently to be deceived about it. He can use the flags for the wind near him, even though they each indicate only a small segment of moving air.

"The mirage is more sensitive than the flags since it has less inertia and momentum. That is why in a light breeze the flags and mirage do not agree momentarily. Perhaps disagreement on these two indicators occurs more frequently when the flags are high above the line of sight and the ground well below . . . [For example] at the Stickledown Range at Bisley, and when there are cross currents in the different strata."

From *Highpower Rifle* by G. David Tubb:

David Tubb writes that he has found mirage easier to learn to read than flags. He says that he does not find mirage helpful in calculating the wind value for his first shot, but he finds it very helpful in identifying that a change is occurring and in recognizing a condition when it returns. He, like others, finds the mirage particularly helpful in detecting the

imminent change in a fishtail. The mirage is the first indicator to show this type of change: the flow slows down, and then the mirage stops moving in a direction and simply shimmers (i.e., it starts to "boil"). Usually, what happens next is that the wind switches and comes from the other direction.

From *Reading the Wind and Coaching Techniques* by M.Sgt. James R. Owens:

Master Sergeant Owens emphasizes that a good spotting scope is required to see mirage early and accurately. We have found this to be not only true but also very important.

He also explains how to use your scope to determine the angle of the wind: turn your scope into the wind until the mirage appears to boil, or rise straight up. The angle at which your scope is pointed is the angle from which the wind is blowing.[22]

Choosing Flags or Mirage

The fact is that you don't choose one over the other, you use both; sometimes alternately and sometimes in concert. It's like having a hammer and a screwdriver; you use the one that's right for the job.

Summary of Tactics for Near/Far Flags/Mirage

- If conditions are uniform the length of the range, any indicator will be accurate.
- If conditions are not uniform the length of the range, use the near indicators to make your basic assessment, and the far indicators to modify it.
- If winds are very light and you are playing for V-bulls, use mirage wherever you can get a good reading.
- If winds are moderate and fairly constant in terms of direction and varying in terms of speed, use both flags and mirage—the mirage to tell you when the change occurs and the flag to tell you how much. The flag should be an upwind flag and near the firing line.
- If winds are direction sensitive (fairly constant in terms of speed), use the nearest upwind flag that will give you a clear reading.

- If winds are very strong, plan to use flags and perhaps trees—but not mirage.

Assessing Size of Bull vs. Wind Spreads

If the bull is 2 minutes and the wind condition has a 1-minute spread, you could decide to just center the group and shoot good shots. The thinking here is that you probably can't read a ½-minute change, and the natural shot distribution of the group will give you just as many V-bulls as twiddling the knobs. (See Using the Shoot-Through Tactic below.)

If the bull is 2 minutes and the wind has a 2-minute spread, and you set the sight in the center, you will sacrifice a lot of little nippers on the outside edge of the line.

If the wind has a 4- or 5-minute spread, the changes are usually loud and clear; you just have to have the courage to make the sight correction.

Using the Shoot-Through Tactic

"I recall a blustery wind varying from 16 to 20 minutes at 900 yards . . . The wind was fluctuating so rapidly that I did not feel capable of coping with it . . . I therefore corrected from my sighters and during the score made no wind changes and totally ignored the indicators and finished with 49!"[23]

Most of us have seen a junior shooter win a very difficult match over far more experienced shooters. The reason is usually because the junior shooter, unable to make sophisticated wind decisions, did the best thing he or she could: centered the group and fired good shots.

When is this the right tactic? Certainly when conditions are beyond our capabilities! And also when the math is right! Take a look at Figure 57.

- In the shoot-through sight setting illustration, shown at the left in Figure 57, you will almost always get a

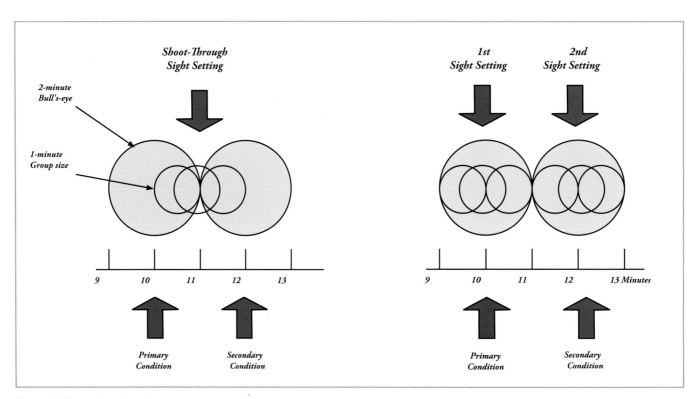

Figure 57. Shoot-through tactic.

bull's-eye, but your odds of getting a V-bull are somewhat reduced.

- In the other scenario, shown at right in Figure 57, where you try to anticipate the conditions, you will always get a bull's-eye and often a V-bull, *when you are at the right setting*. However, when you miss a wind change, you are guaranteed an inner.

"[In a fishtailing wind, it is] best NOT to set zero . . . because the zero . . . wind time may be so short you could never catch it. Better to choose one side, and set the sight about two-thirds of the worst you think it can get. That way you get two chances close together, once rising towards maximum, and again falling away."[24]

Assessing Primary and Secondary Conditions

Just prior to your match, you complete the final details of your on-site range recce. Recall the "overall procedure" and the "thought process for your first sighter" outlined in chapter 2. Once you have a mental picture of the airflow, you can start to identify the primary and secondary conditions.

The primary condition is the condition that is most often present, and usually it is the one that lasts the longest and that all other conditions return to. The secondary condition is the next most common condition. Occasionally, you may be able to identify a third and (rarely) a fourth condition.

Most often, though, there are two conditions, and everything else is simply moving toward one or the other of these. When you are shooting single string, you can use the smallbore technique of shooting only one condition and waiting through the others until your primary condition returns. When you are firing alternately in pairs or in threesomes, you must recognize each of these conditions, adjust the sight to the known setting for that condition, and fire when it is your turn.

In the diagram below, you can see that the primary condition lasts for about 4 minutes of the 12-minute pattern, and the secondary condition is less well defined and lasts only about 2 minutes.

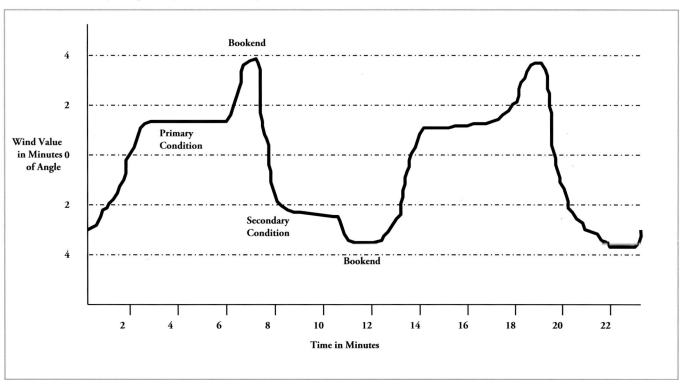

Figure 58. Primary and secondary conditions.

The rest of the time (half of the cycle) is spent with the wind moving toward or away from these two conditions. If you focused your shooting tactics around having either the primary or the secondary setting on your sights (about 1½ minutes right and about 2¼ minutes left), you would probably shoot a solid score for the conditions. (Notice that the shoot-through tactic would not work in this situation, because the difference between the two conditions [about 3¾ minutes] is greater than the diameter of the bull.)

Bookending

This is a technique that we often use, especially in intimidating winds. It simply means that you identify the minimum and maximum conditions (or the furthest left and the furthest right conditions, in a switching wind). This gives you the confidence to identify the worst-case condition and estimate its effect. Then you can conclude that all other conditions will fall inside these "bookends." If you think the wind is up, move the sight setting to 1 minute from the upper end; when it is down, stay within 1 minute of the low end.

For example, in Figure 58 the bookend outside of the secondary condition is at about 3¾ minutes left and lasts over one minute in time. Under target rifle rules (i.e., your shot must be fired in a 45-second time period), you may have to shoot this condition. If you were anticipating the secondary condition and had your sights set at 2¼ minutes left, you would simply add an extra minute or so and fire your shot.

Using Four Data Points

If you have identified the primary and secondary conditions within the bookends, you now have four data points that can be used to set your sights. In most conditions, this is enough information to place a shot in the bull most of the time. For example, Figure 59 shows a 10- to 20-MOA spread (a windy shoot!). You can identify the following conditions and their appropriate sight settings:

* The high-end bookend is 20 MOA.
* The primary condition is at about the 16-minute mark.

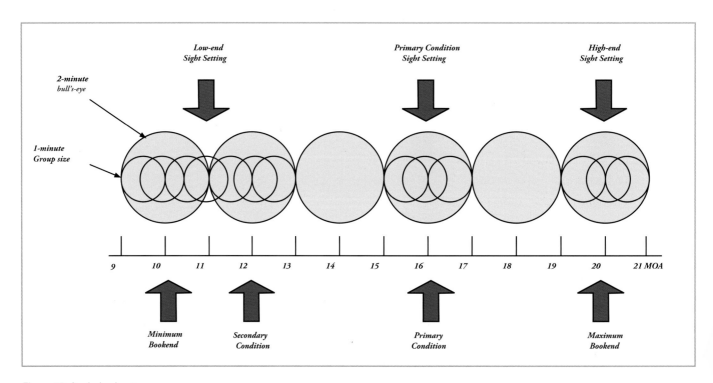

Figure 59. A windy shoot.

• The secondary condition is a "let-off" to about 12 MOA, and the lowest bookend is about 10 MOA, so you could now reasonably assess a low-end setting of 11 minutes to cover both.

Therefore, you would be using a primary condition sight setting of 16 MOA, going to 20 MOA when the wind is stronger, and going to 11 MOA when it lets off. All you need is the courage to change the sights and the speed to get the shot off while your condition is still present.

Even an intimidating wind condition of 10 to 20 minutes can submit to analysis, and while it's still not easy to shoot well, having a plan improves your chances of predicting the right sight setting and steeling your nerve to make big sight changes!

Using Linda's "Sandbox" Tactic

In estimating the effect the wind will have on the deflection of the bullet as it flies through the air, a significant factor is "value," or the angle at which the wind approaches the bullet.

It is intuitively obvious that a strong crosswind will have a far greater effect than a tailwind of the same speed. What is less apparent is that the crosswind effect shows up earlier than you might expect; in fact, when the wind is blowing from 11 or 1 o'clock, it has already acquired half its crosswind force. (See chapter 1, "Wind Basics.") Subsequently, although it is often easier to notice a speed change, it is often more important to recognize a value, or direction, change.

Linda keeps a simple chart or diagram with her for each distance. When she assesses the book-end conditions for the match, she will mark them on the chart to see what the spread of settings will be. In the example shown in Figure 60, the conditions are "moderate" to "fresh" winds (about 15 to 25 kph, or 10 to 15 mph) from 2 to 3 o'clock.[25] Note that the difference between the 2 and 3 o'clock setting is smaller than the V-bull (from 3 to 3½ MOA for a "moderate"

wind; from 4¼ to 5 MOA for a "fresh" wind). However, the difference between the "moderate" and "fresh" settings is almost greater than the bull (from 3 to 4¼ MOA when the wind is blowing from 2 o'clock; from 3½ to 5 MOA when the wind is blowing from 3 o'clock). Therefore, Linda will focus on the speed of the wind as the key determinant of her sight settings.

In Figure 61 we show the same situation, but using a more visual tool. We laminate our diagrams so that we can draw on them with a grease pencil during the matches.[26] We mark an X to highlight the conditions we expect. In this case, we are expecting "moderate" and "fresh" winds from 2 and 3 o'clock. We can easily see that a sight setting of about 3½ will deal with the "moderate" wind, and a setting of about 5¼ will accommodate the "fresh" wind condition.

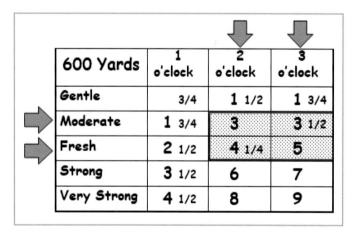

600 Yards	1 o'clock	2 o'clock	3 o'clock
Gentle	3/4	1 1/2	1 3/4
Moderate	1 3/4	3	3 1/2
Fresh	2 1/2	4 1/4	5
Strong	3 1/2	6	7
Very Strong	4 1/2	8	9

Figure 60. Linda's "sandbox" tactic—chart.

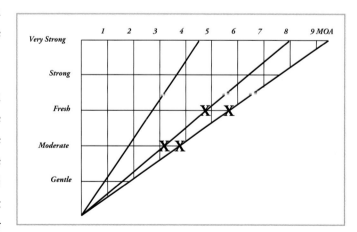

Figure 61. Linda's "sandbox" tactic—diagram.

Using Your Rate of Fire as a Tactic

Just in case you thought rate of fire was a technique only for single-string matches, here's what target rifle shooter Des Burke had to say: "Timing also becomes an important tactic. The marksman should learn to fire rapidly . . . It pays sometimes to ignore the demands of . . . clerical records and to concentrate on speed . . ."[27]

The British are now training all their team shooters to release the shot within five seconds of the "go on" command, and many of them do it within two or three seconds. It is just as important for an individual competitor to be able to release a good shot fast. Even when you shoot alternately, being able to release the shot quickly will improve your rhythm (an important factor in firing perfect shots) and allow you to stay in step with the wind (an important factor in catching your wind condition). The shorter you make the overall match (by firing quickly), the better the odds that you will get to fire as many shots in one condition as possible. Even if you must fire in several conditions, you are more likely to finish the match while the overall pattern you identified is still present.

SHOT-BY-SHOT TACTICS

These tactics and techniques are focused around the efforts you make for a specific shot. If you have organized your pre-match preparation and selected the best game plan, these shot-by-shot tactics should mostly be a way of addressing the circumstances of the particular moment when you must fire your shot.

Watching the Wind to the Last Second

If possible, it is a great advantage to be able to watch your wind indicator while you are in the aim. This is an advantage that shooters using telescopic sights enjoy at all times.

For shooters who are using iron sights, it is an advantage that they should strive to achieve. If you are watching mirage through a spotting scope, set the scope so that you can see the mirage just by raising an eyebrow or changing your mental focus.[28]

If you are watching flags and can set up your position so that you can see a significant flag while you are in the aim, do so. When the conditions are exactly right, you can turn your attention to the sight picture and fire your shot.

Linda recalls having Pat Vamplew watch her shooting 800 yards at Winona Range in Ontario, Canada. He watched her take maximum time on a shot and then remarked about her being lucky, because the flag direction changed three times while she was in the aim and she still got a bull's-eye. Actually, she was able to watch a direction flag while in the aim and waited until it came back to her condition before firing.

Using Shot-by-Shot Timing as a Tactic

Often your shot-by-shot timing is determined by match conditions, but when you have some leeway, you can use it to your advantage.

"Once the wind has been judged and set, waste no time getting the shot away. Stop only if you sense conditions have changed significantly. The faster the wind changes:

- The shorter the time you should take to shoot after deciding to fire the shot, and
- The more likely it is that you can wait for the wind to suit the sight settings."[29]

We agree with the above wholeheartedly; however, the shooter needs to be wary of unstable air: "A firer should delay a bit after a sudden change to allow eddies and whorls to settle down. He should remember that the flags have more inertia and momentum than the mirage, and because of this there will be times of disagreement."[30]

These two opinions (above) are also reflected in disagreements among shooters about whether to shoot when the mirage is in a boil. We would likely all agree to avoid shooting in unstable air or when indicators are not keeping up with changes. When the boil is a short-lived condition that the wind passes through on its way to another more stable condition, then firing in the boil produces some problems. However, when the boil is a stable, lasting condition, it can produce a beautiful shoot. The shooter must decide which situation he is dealing with in order to decide whether or not to shoot during the boil.

Being "with" the Wind

Many shooters have had the experience of being "with" the wind, of feeling as though they were part of the wind, like a good dance partner, anticipating every step and swerve and whirl.

Here are some of the sensitivities you need to acquire to enjoy that feeling more often:

- Using the overall wind pattern that you observed and recorded before your match, anticipate the wind's next change.
- Stay engaged and intently focused on the wind during your entire match. Don't let your attention waver for a moment. Watch, remember, and anticipate.
- "Body feel" is important, but remember that if the wind is coming toward you, it is already old news by the time it gets to you. If it's coming from behind, take full advantage: you are getting advance notice of what will soon be moving down the range.
- David Tubb says that he stays ahead of the wind by making aggressive corrections. He likes to shoot during the buildup, and he would rather have his group forming on the upwind side of center during a buildup. He says he can see an increase in wind more easily than he can see a decrease.[31]

Going Off Your Last Shot

This is another technique that can be very useful, mostly for single-string shooting, particularly if you have relatively stable conditions and fast target-marking service.

You simply correct off your last shot and, if conditions have not changed significantly, fire quickly with the corrected

settings. F-Class shooters often use this technique (even when shooting two-to-a-mound), spotting their partner's last shot through their optic sight and then using the "aiming-off" technique to correct from both their own and their partner's last shots.

Usually in target rifle shooting, too much time passes as the shooters alternate. However, Des Burke raised an interesting point in *Canadian Bisley Shooting*. He noted that sometimes the conditions are just so tough to read that everyone is missing the bull, and at that point the shooter must conclude that the indicators are just not providing good information. Under those circumstances, he suggests that using your last shot may introduce less error than using the usual indicators:

> In the cases of very strong winds, the low scores across the range show that the indicators have reached the level where judgment of them is not very accurate, and one may well conclude that the use of the position of one's last shot may introduce less error than the false judgment of the other indicators.
>
> A more hazardous procedure is to use the position of another's shots. This would be doubly so when a shooter does not know what changes, if any, have been made or whether these changes were too little or excessive. If a beginner has the good fortune to be squadded with a group of experts, the extent to which they are caught by sudden changes while on aim may provide a clue. In cases of a sudden serious change, it is well to glance along the whole line of shot positions and get a statistically significant idea of its magnitude.[32]

Many shooters do use the tactic of going off the placement of others' shots. If you notice that several or many of the shooters on your part of the range have just had wide wind shots (while you are watching conditions that they didn't see because they were firing), you can use their shot fall to gauge the size of the change. You simply correct to compensate for their error. Some shooters take the full correction, and some take half of it. Others simply use this as an indication that they should go with the high end of their own estimate. You don't know, of course, what correction those shooters already had put on their sights and whether the condition that put their shots out will still exist when you are firing.

Using Your Plot

There is considerable skill required in correctly interpreting your graph and your Plot-o-Matic (EZ-Graf). One well-respected British shooter told us that he doesn't graph, because it tells you only the errors of the past without offering any constructive forecast for the future.

We believe that the Plot-o-Matic (EZ-Graf) helps you visualize patterns of wind and therefore helps you anticipate the possible conditions in which you will be shooting your next shot. If you can't quite get a grip on the wind, just go to the Plot-o-Matic (EZ-Graf)—or your graph—and notice the high-end setting and the low-end setting that would have gotten you into the bull's-eye. If there's an intermediate setting required, note that, too. Then just go off the Plot-o-Matic (EZ-Graf).

- If the wind is strong, use the high-end setting.
- If the wind is soft, use the low-end setting.
- If it's somewhere in between, use the intermediate setting.

It's not the most glamorous tactic, but it will likely keep you in the black better than any other technique, when you are otherwise lost.

And When You're Really in Trouble . . .

This final tactic is intended to rescue a shoot that has gone completely off the rails. If you think you need to start over, then start over. Go back to the thought process that you used to make the wind call for your initial sighter.

Step 1: Observe conditions.
Step 2: Convert conditions to sight settings.
Step 3: Make your wind call and set your sights.
Step 4: Fire and call the shot.
Step 5: Record and analyze results.

Alain Marion vividly demonstrated the value of this tactic at the 2003 national matches at Connaught Ranges in Canada. The wind came up dramatically just prior to the start of the Governor General's finals. Until then, only a modest point spread separated the leaders, and Alain led in the qualifying aggregate by a single point. It really was anyone's to win.

Alain fired an inner (score of four out of five points) on his first sighter and an inner on his second sighter. On his next six shots, he lost five points. And then he decided to change his tactics.

Instead of trying to relate one shot to the next, he started to treat each shot as a first sighter. He would look at the conditions, assess them, and select a sight setting. This tactic won him the match and the coveted Governor General's Medal by a whopping five points.

SUMMARY

Every shooting opportunity, whether practice or match, is an opportunity to develop your tactical skills. If the conditions call for a technique that you already have in your toolbox, call it out and practice your ability to use it well. If the conditions call for a technique that you do not yet possess, design a tool and test it.

CHAPTER 4

UNDERLYING SKILLS

"One's ultimate success depends on one's own meticulous self-analysis . . .
—Desmond T. Burke

The ultimate skill that we all want to acquire is the ability to "read the wind," but this is made up of several individual skills, such as observation and memorization. We believe that each individual skill can be learned and practiced, both on and off the range.

Off the range, you can easily practice paying attention to the wind, describing its pattern, assessing its value, and estimating your sight settings . . . take your wind meter with you when you take the dog for a walk or go shopping.

On the range, one of the best ways to get good as a wind reader is to spend time as a wind coach. We use the classic team setup to train our students in wind reading.

- The shooter's job is simply to fire a perfect shot.
- The plotter's job is to keep the group centered and, by keeping a record of shot fall, to assist in identifying wind conditions.
- The wind coach's job is to focus completely on the process of reading the wind and determining the correct sight setting for each condition.

In Figure 62, you can see the team setup we used during our competition rifle course in Florida in 2003, which was hosted by the Bermuda Rifle Team.

- As a wind coach, you never have to take your eyes off the wind; this will improve your observation skills.
- If the wind changes during shot execution, you will see it. This will improve the accuracy of the feedback you are getting while you are building your sense of cause and effect, and in the long run will improve your ability to identify critical factors and analyze shot placement.

Figure 62. Plotter, wind coach, shooter.

- Many wind coaches have told us that by practicing in this way, their decision-making skills improve. They think it's because they are forced to separate the wind call from shot execution. They don't hedge their bets, riding on one side of the bull or the other; they always try to make a fully centered call. Because making the wind call is their only job, they do it better. The effect is carried over into their own shooting.

- Your confidence (and your ability to take risks) will improve as you develop your skill. If you have the opportunity to be part of a large team-coaching situation, where you are "wired for sound," do it! In this type of situation, the coaches are joined together by intercom, along with a central (lead) coach, to talk together about the wind calls they are making. This is a particularly good way to learn from other people's wind calls and probably the only opportunity you will have to compare your wind reading with that of others.

We believe that improving your ability to perform these underlying skills will improve your ability to read the wind. One of Canada's top shooters (and one of the top shooters in the world) is Alain Marion. He acknowledges that he has very good eyesight. This undoubtedly helps him in delivering an excellent shot, because he is very sure of his sight picture. But we believe that it also helps him observe the indicators that

will contribute to his wind decision. His superior eyesight has made him more sensitive to these indicators than someone who sees the world less clearly. Now, you can't practice to get better eyesight, but you sure can practice to put more attention into observing the details of the indicators!

IDENTIFYING THE CRITICAL FACTORS

More than any other skill, this is perhaps the one that separates the champions from the rest. It is the ability to identify and focus on the critical factors, and to dismiss and ignore the noncritical ones.

Some time ago, we wrote an article for *Tactical Shooter* magazine entitled "How Good Shooters Think," based on research conducted by Edward F. Etzel Jr. as a part of his master of science in physical education at West Virginia University. His findings were published in the *Journal of Sport Psychology* (1979) under the title "Validation of a Conceptual Model Characterizing Attention among International Rifle Shooters."

Etzel identified the following skills and tested rifle shooters to measure which skills were most important:

1. Duration, the ability to think/concentrate for an extended period
2. Capacity, the ability to think about complex things
3. Flexibility, the ability to change the focus or topic of thought easily
4. Intensity, the ability to be alert and focus intently on a subject
5. Selectivity, the ability to focus on only the few things that are directly relevant to the task at hand

What Etzel found was that, of all the attention skills that he tested, by far the most important was selectivity, "the ability to discriminately perceive relevant information, as well as the ability to screen out irrelevant information." Research has generally indicated that human beings are extremely limited in this ability. Since selectivity is a rare skill and it is the most important skill identified in Etzel's study, it is possibly the defining skill for champion shooters.[1]

The purpose of identifying the critical factors is to make your analysis as simple and as accurate as possible. This brings out the principle of "keep it simple." During competition, it is essential that you identify the smallest number of things that you need to pay attention to so that you can focus your attention on the right things.

One of the ways you can train to identify critical factors is to watch other people shoot. For example, if you see a flag movement (e.g., the safety flag at the butts) that results in shots being blown off, you may have found a critical factor.

Another way to identify critical factors is to talk to people who know the range to find out which of the indicators they believe are the most critical to watch.

A third way is to do a postmortem analysis of your match (preferably with your coach) to identify which factors you used and which you missed and need to use next time.

OBSERVATION SKILLS

"The marksman must develop an accurate mental picture of the wind indicators and the ability to remember it from shot to shot."[2]

The purpose of training observation skills is purely to improve your ability to see the details of the wind indicators. At this point, you don't care about the wind value in minutes or your sight settings; you are simply training to observe the initial condition accurately and to see the changes.

If you are a visually oriented person, you may be able to take a mental "snapshot" of, for example, a flag's position and perhaps record your observation with a little drawing. However, if you are a verbally oriented person, you may need to record a verbal memory, such as "the tip of the flag is an apparent finger width above the tree line." The point is that

you must find your own way to ensure that you have fully appreciated the indicator.

In some cases, you need to find ways to make the indicator more vivid to your brain, so you focus on what sets it apart from the rest of the scenery. In other cases, you need to focus your attitude: when you see a flag change from 12 to 1 o'clock, it should scream at you the way a red traffic light hollers "stop!"

If you're interested in observation as a human skill, search the Internet under "visual perception" or "psychology cognition"; there's a lot of ongoing research in this field, attempting to figure out how we humans acquire, process, and act on visual stimuli.

Observing Flags

To fully observe a flag or other wind indicator, you need to see, recognize, and appreciate the details of the flag.

- Observe the tip of the flag as it relates to the flagpole or a reference point such as a distant horizon—this gives you a detailed reference from which to note changes.
- Notice the centerline of the flag, and the angle it makes to the flagpole—as the wind speed increases, so does the angle.
- Appreciate the number of ripples in the main body of the flag, as well as in the tip—even after the flag angle is 90 degrees from the pole, the flag will continue to flatten out (ripples become smaller, and there are more of them) as the wind speed increases. Along the same lines, look at the softness or stiffness of the flag—more wind makes the flag stiffer. See how the base end of the flag arches away from the pole, straining against its mounting rope—when the flag is showing maximum wind speed, you can see subtle differences in the way the flag strains against its mooring.
- If the flag is near you, you can sometimes hear the flap of the cloth in the wind—the louder it flaps, the stronger the wind.

To train your flag observation skills, start by taking every opportunity to be on the range where you can see wind flags. Bring your wind meter and your notepad with you. Observe the flags, seeing all the details mentioned above, and relate them to the speed indicated by the wind meter. Practice deciding what speed each flag represents. If you feel a wind change, or if your wind meter detects one, notice and record the change in the flags. The purpose of this exercise is to improve your ability to see and recognize the subtle changes in the flags when wind conditions change.

Take pictures of flags that represent various wind speeds and wind directions. Compare the pictures to the flag diagrams you use. Practice observing the details of the flags and categorizing the wind they represent.

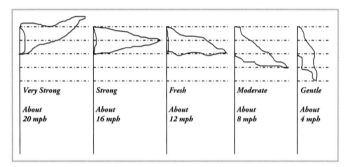

Figure 63a. Observing flags—diagrams.

Figure 63b. Observing flags—pictures.

In addition to noting the flags you are using for wind speed, you need also to notice the flag that you are using for wind direction. You can sharpen your observations by drawing a little sketch of the range and its flags, and then calculating the angles of the flags that you might use for direction. Recall that your wind direction flag is one that is blowing straight away or straight toward you.

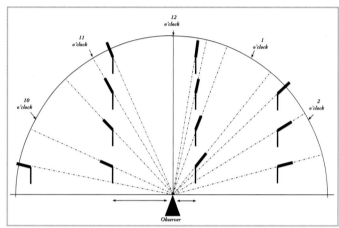

Figure 64. Range diagram.

In the range diagram (Figure 64), you can see that the flags that are nearer to 12 o'clock will give you directional readings that are closer to 12 o'clock. Notice also that a row of flags that is very near your line of sight gives you a steeper angle than flags that are farther to your left or right.

To train your angle observation skills, pick a flag that is flying straight away from you and watch it for a while. Note which side of the pole the flag moves toward and then notice the details of how much of the flag is showing on that side—the more of the flag that is showing, the greater the direction change. (See Figure 65.) Use your range diagram to estimate the angle toward which the flag has moved.

Observing Mirage

It seems that almost everyone experiences mirage a little differently. Most people cannot describe what they see in any detail. Usually, if you ask for a description, you get something like, "It's the heat waves. You know, the air moving." Actually, that's pretty much what it is!

The mirage that we shooters refer to is the same kind of mirage that produces images of distant ships floating over the

Figure 65. Observing flag direction changes.

water. It is created by the same type of light refraction, caused by light traveling through layers of air that are at different temperatures. The interesting thing is that the mirage we watch is a mirage of the air itself. And because wind is air in motion, we "see" the wind in the mirage.

As we mentioned in chapter 1, most people describe five basic mirage formations:

1. Boiling: 0 to 1 mph
2. Leaning: 1 to 3 mph
3. Flowing gently: 4 to 7 mph
4. Flowing rapidly: 8 to 11 mph
5. Streaming to flatlining: 12 mph and more (but not much more)

Sophisticated mirage readers report they are able to distinguish several stages between "flowing gently" and "flowing rapidly," which gives them more detailed wind estimates. Others, and some very good shooters among them, say that they can discern only three stages: "boiling," "flowing gently," and "flatlining." Several of the people we consulted in preparing this book indicated that their best use of mirage is only to assess direction, and especially early warning for direction changes in light winds—only because, for them, it is hard to see changes in the faster mirage. (See Figure 66.)

As with learning to observe the details of the flags, the shooter needs to take every opportunity to set up his spotting scope and watch mirage—you don't need to be at a range to do this—any open field, yard, or parking lot where you can see mirage will do. As with the flags, find the primary condition and recognize its detailed characteristics. For many people, the way to really see mirage is to attempt to draw the mirage, noting the amplitude and frequency of the waves. When your wind meter tells you that the wind has increased, notice how the amplitude and frequency of the waves have changed.

Try to find a way of describing the mirage that makes sense to you. If you are a fly fisherman, perhaps descriptions that you'd use to describe a trout stream would be helpful. Or, as

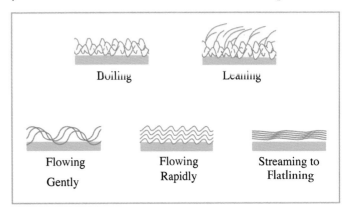

Figure 66. Observing mirage.

65

one shooter who is familiar with syrups told us he describes the mirage in terms of the heaviness of syrup. We have also heard shooters describe mirage in terms of the number of "bumps" in the waves across the top of the target frame.

One thing we cannot overemphasize: the scope you use to view mirage is very important. It's no accident that the national teams from many countries use enormous astronomical telescopes. To see mirage as soon as it is present is a competitive advantage, and to see its details clearly is equally important.

RECORDING AND RECORD KEEPING

Good record keeping and administrative procedures are required to ensure that you are working with facts. If you have moved your sight and not recorded it on your plot, or if you incorrectly mark the shot position on your target replica, you will not be able to analyze the situation properly. Even the accuracy of your target replica for your particular rifle system (sight radius and rear sight movement being the keys) is part of the overall accuracy of the information you will be using to analyze shot placement.

We have seen otherwise careful shooters plot their shots ¼ to ½ minute out of position.

There is a strong tendency to plot a shot near a scoring ring, either just outside or just inside the ring. One way to counteract this tendency is to look at the shot indicator in terms of how it lines up with the edges of two scoring rings.

And yes, these small errors can make a big difference. If you don't remember, take another look at the diagrams that show "grouping high in the bull" (Figure 54) and "grouping slightly high and slightly left" (Figure 55). Small plotting errors can produce the same effect as a poorly centered group—only you won't necessarily be able to see it.

A final check of your accuracy is this: when you finish the match, record the settings on your sight and check reality against the record you kept. If you finish within ¼ minute on vernier sights, you are doing well. On telescopic sights with easy-to-read scales, we expect an exact match.

MEMORIZING

The purpose of memorizing the condition is to enable you to compare one condition to the next when conditions are changing and to recognize when a condition returns.

This is where recognizing the primary condition really comes into play. It is simpler to be looking for one or two specific conditions—and recognize all the rest as exceptions or variants of the known conditions—rather than to try to keep an image of all possible conditions.

To improve your recall and your ability to recognize patterns, you can make a record of the conditions by drawing little diagrams or making notes using word pictures. Our preference is to have templates (like the flag diagrams shown in Figure 63a) that we can match to conditions. We find it easier, for example, to say that a given flag looks like the "fresh" flag (its tip level with the base of the hoist) than to try to estimate the angle of the flag from the pole ("looks like 57 degrees").

There are some basic indicators and conditions you should master first:

- The five flag velocities
    ○ Gentle
    ○ Moderate
    ○ Fresh
    ○ Strong
    ○ Very strong
- The four flag directions
    ○ 12 o'clock
    ○ 1 o'clock
    ○ 2 o'clock
    ○ 3 o'clock
- The five mirage patterns
    ○ Boiling

- º Leaning
- º Flowing gently
- º Flowing rapidly
- º Streaming or flatlining

Once you've mastered the basics, you can start working toward increasing the level of detail. There are three techniques that will help your ability to memorize:

- Identify patterns.
- Match conditions to known patterns.
- Look for exceptions.

When you are first learning to read the wind, strive to identify, memorize, and recognize a single condition. Then learn one more and add it to your repertoire. Focus on what you do know, apply it, and learn more. Gradually you will build your own personal database of experience, and gradually you will move from novice to master.

As Reynolds and Fulton wrote in *Target Rifle Shooting,* the shooter must use his own judgment based on visual cues about what the wind is really doing. There is no instrument that he can use to measure what the wind is doing to the bullet as it travels along its trajectory. There is no easy way to learn how to read the wind; there is no substitute for experience. Top shooters are often able to assess the wind conditions and make judgments with remarkable accuracy. "The best that a beginner can expect to do is to learn and memorize the known effect of certain defined wind forces, and make a reasonable guess at the prevailing wind's strength and direction."[3]

ANALYZING SHOT PLACEMENT

The purpose of analyzing shot placement is to ensure that you understand why the shot landed where it did so that you can correct the right factor. When a shot does not go where you expected it to, any of the following factors can be the cause:

- Technical capability of your rifle and ammunition
- Your ability to fire a perfect shot

- Your ability to "call" a less-than-perfect shot
- Your ability to center the group
- Your sight setting
- The effect of the wind

You need to understand the technical capability of your equipment to appreciate its grouping capability—shots that are within the grouping capability cannot be assessed for wind effects. If you can consistently fire a perfect shot (within the technical capability of your equipment), you will vastly improve your ability to establish the effect of wind versus the effect of your shooting ability.

Whenever your shot is less than perfect, you need to be able to "call your shot" (i.e., recognize an error in the sight picture at the moment the shot is fired and anticipate where the shot will land) so that you can discount the error in the sight picture (including canting errors) before you attempt to calculate any wind effect. In addition to understanding the grouping capability of your system (you, your rifle, and your ammunition), you need to have the group as perfectly centered as possible.

And, finally, you need to be sure of your sight setting (including your wind zero) before you can start to analyze the effect of the wind on your shot placement. Correcting most of these is beyond the scope of this book, yet they are prerequisites to being able to effectively call the wind.

DECISION MAKING

The purpose of the decision-making skill is to be able to produce a correct outcome, using a defensible (and repeatable) method.

Often, the shooter will get lulled into an "easy shoot" and stop making decisions altogether! Or sometimes a bit of panic or wishful thinking will make the shooter leap to a conclusion without using a clear decision-making process. And, in hard conditions, sometimes the shooter will come to the right conclusion (e.g., a 6-minute sight correction) but lack the confidence in his decision-making process to follow through and make the change on his sights.

The best way to make sure that you are always making good decisions is always to follow a solid decision-making process. The following thought process (detailed in chapter 2) is a good place to start:

- Is the wind the same or different?
- Has the wind increased in value or decreased?
- Is the change a little or a lot?

Your ability to observe and memorize will bear strongly on the quality of the information you bring to the decision-making process. And if you follow the same thought process each time, you will improve your chances of making the correct wind call.

FOLLOWING YOUR HUNCHES

There is "an intuitive sixth sense that a shooter develops with experience wherein he consciously or unconsciously recalls similar experiences and just 'knows' [what he needs to do]."[4] Learning to trust your intuition can be a challenge, especially for those of us who are naturally analytical and live life very consciously.

We all have a sixth sense that has at times caused us to make a decision just because it felt right. Reading the wind is a complex skill that involves all parts of the brain, including the most mysterious parts. Your body can know something that you cannot articulate. You make a good decision that you cannot explain. We sometimes call this following a hunch.

Following a hunch is not the same as sloppy thinking. Sloppy thinking means accepting an inferior set of facts or an inferior decision process. Following a hunch is based on good data and good process, plus something more that you can't define right at the moment.

Following your hunches won't make you right all the time, but the more you practice it, the better you will get. Hunches that are based on both conscious and subconscious facts can give you better decisions than either one alone.

"If you see some apparently variable factor arise . . . the chances are that any intelligent attempt to make allowances for those changed circumstances will probably be better for your results than doing nothing at all . . . if you see/feel/sense/suspect the wind has changed enough to take you out, the worst thing you can do is to ignore your gut feelings. Better by far for your next bullet's chances to do something, pretty much anything, by way of a sensible adjustment in the right direction."[5]

COURAGE, RISK TAKING, AND CONFIDENCE

Perhaps the best way to describe courage is the feeling that you get when you make your first 5-minute sight change and go from "bull" to "bull." Many points have been lost because shooters were caught in a comfort zone, and while they may have seen changes that were outside that comfort zone, they could not force themselves to leave it and make a bigger sight correction. Sometimes a shooter who is uncertain about making a change will make half of the correction or will make a correction that is inside the group showing on his graph or Plot-o-Matic (EZ-Graf), even though the wind is clearly showing a new and stronger condition. We are not talking about tactics here—we are talking about having the courage of your convictions!

The following are a few ways to develop your courage and confidence:

- Armchair analysis after your shoot. As you debrief your match with your coach, identify all the opportunities you had to make a more aggressive wind call and assess what difference that might have made.
- "Attaboys" for overcorrection versus undercorrection—since the vast majority of our incorrect wind calls are undercalls, reward yourself for having the courage to

make the perfect call and reward yourself for the next best situation, the overcalled shot.

- Pretend it's your first sighter. When faced with a major change, especially one outside your bookends, pretend that you are making your first sighter and focus on all the factors you would use to decide your sight setting at the beginning of the match—and then have the courage to listen to yourself.

- Pretend it's a practice. Too often, we focus on "not losing points" instead of learning how to make center shots, especially since many of us rarely get a genuine practice opportunity. Sometimes we need to keep the importance of winning a given match in perspective and favor our learning opportunity by taking a risk that we otherwise would not.

And on that last point, remember the quotation from Des Burke, when he shot a 49 by having the courage to leave his sights alone in hard conditions? Well, here's the entire passage:

I recall a blustery wind varying from 16 to 20 minutes at 900 yards . . . The wind was fluctuating so rapidly that I did not feel capable of coping with it . . . I therefore corrected from my sighters and during the score made no wind changes and totally ignored the indicators and finished with 49! The fact that it was a practice probably made such a course easier to follow.[6]

SUMMARY

Of all the skills we have discussed, most experienced shooters would emphasize the importance of these two:

- Observation
- Memorization

The ability to observe the details of the conditions in the flags and mirage and any other indicators is a fundamental requirement for learning to read the wind. This really is a matter of practice: the more often you observe in an attentive way, the more sensitive you will become to details.

The ability to memorize and recall your observations is the next most critical skill that a shooter can develop. Certainly this is more challenging to some people than to others, but all of us can work on memory skills simply by exercising them.

CHAPTER 5

WORDS OF WISDOM

Authors' note: As discussed in the preface, we originally started writing a story about reading the wind for Precision Shooting magazine. We started with a simple idea ... how do you think about reading the wind? We came up with a simple thought process that we feel is pretty effective. But then we wanted to add some techniques and tactics, and then, because we believe that these things are all completely "learnable," we had to put in something about the underlying skills.

Somewhere, in the midst of all that, the entire story became completely unmanageable. Keith suggested that we stop struggling and just treat it like a short book instead of a long story. So we did. We added a chapter on basics. Then we thought about what else we wish we had known before we had started competitive shooting at long range and decided to add a chapter of "words of wisdom," wind-reading thoughts from some of our best long-range shooters.

We decided to gather this information from any excellent wind readers and started by canvassing the members of the Dominion of Canada Rifle Association (DCRA) Hall of Fame, as well as top shooters from the United Kingdom, the United States, Australia, South Africa, and elsewhere. Some of these top shooters were recommended by their national rifle associations, while others were recommended by PALMA Team coaches, and still other individuals we contacted directly. We explained our situation to them and asked them specifically for their help:

> "It's in the last chapter, 'Words of Wisdom" that we need your help. What we'd like to include is your thought process . . . what do you think about when you are reading the wind? What do you wish you had known about 'wind thinking' before you started competitive shooting at long range?
>
> "We're looking for a few paragraphs (or so) on your thought process and perhaps a short example of a time it really contributed to a successful performance."

The rest of this chapter is the result of what we received from these esteemed shooters, and their advice is told in their own words. That is, while the other chapters in this book are told from our perspective, the remainder of this chapter is written from the perspective of the guest authors who contributed these words of wisdom. We are forever indebted to the shooters who shared their thoughts with all of us. It was certainly not easy for all of them to put their thoughts down, and we are touched by their efforts on our behalf. As George Chase said, "What you are about to receive from shooters around the world should make for an interesting read." Indeed.

EDUARDO ABRIL DE FONTCUBERTA, SPAIN
KING OF 2 MILES

Dealing with Wind at Extreme Long-Range Shooting

Shooting past one mile[1] is what the Extreme Long Range (ELR) community has recently agreed as true ELR. There was a lot of argument about the real challenges involved and how to set a threshold that we could call "ELR." Most of the ELR leaders agree that once a certain caliber goes into the transonic zone, a new set of external ballistics *unknowns* come into play, be it 700 yards for a 30-30, or 3000 yards for a .375 CheyTac.

For most modern shooters, obtaining an accurate fire solution at 1000 yards is not a problem, thanks to the latest developments in ballistics software and measuring equipment. Distance to the target, meteorological conditions (MET), and environmental conditions (ENV) such as shooting angle, are not unknowns anymore.

There seems to be a new sense of confidence that comes from how easy is to obtain a good fire solution using these new tools. The problem is that once this over-confident fire solution hits a certain range, high hit ratios drop radically, and misses become the norm.

If you are reading this book, then you are motivated enough to face the challenges of shooting past one mile and to try to understand what is involved in increasing that hit ratio to an acceptable point. Don't believe those false Gurus out there on YouTube making claims of a cold bore 4000-yard shot. We are not yet ready for that; just check the King of 2 Miles (Ko2M) scores.

To achieve those ELR hits we first need to better understand the little-known factors that are affecting our bullet's point of impact. Some of these factors come from the internal ballistics like bore compression, from the external ballistics like aerodynamic jump or hyper stable flight, or from our environment (like the wind).

What We Know

Right now, we have a good set of measuring equipment available that remove from the unknowns some of the critical factors that affect our shooting. We now measure muzzle velocity (MV) with ease with Magnetospeed magnetic chronographs and LabRadars, or use the huge BC (ballistic coefficient) libraries available from manufacturers, which are more accurate that most might want to admit.

We even have custom drag curves from several ballistic solution manufacturers such as Hornady, Lapua and Bryan Litz (Applied Ballistics) that allow us a high impact ratio with little effort, but only for some bullets they have custom profiled.

Kestrel has brought full meteorological station capabilities to the shooters and Vectronix's laser range finders are widespread at ELR firing lines.

We have new hardware such as TACOM HQ Charlie optics, Ivey adjustable mounts, superb new riflescopes designed for ELR such as Schmidt und Bender 5-45x56 and also new calibers, new barrel twists and new bullets. So, are we ready for pushing the envelope?

What We Don't Know

This is when the story gets interesting. With the above *knowns and hardware,* we have enough data to work reliably up to 1000 or 1200 yards with a very high hit ratio. If we use the latest hardware we can increase that a little more, but as soon as we get close to a mile and require cold bore shots, or repeated hits, the misses will start to add up. Why?

Just check the World Record attempt at the 2018 Shot Show and you will find that some of the best shooters in the World struggled to get past one mile if required to hit 3 out of 3 on a cold bore. And think about the superb work by Nate Stalter from David Tubb´s team that came in with the record with 2011 yards, and check the equipment they had, as this configuration, with a Magnetospeed permanently installed and an advanced thermal camera so the spotter could see the bullet trace, tells you a lot about what we are facing.

You would have expected more, wouldn't you? This is our reality check.

In my humble opinion, we are struggling at 2000 yards when required to hit cold bore because we still need more refinement in our software solutions and because of the great unknown: the wind.

Ballistics software is a key component of our ELR arsenal, if not the single one most important and critical. Without software, it's virtually impossible to succeed in ELR , so try to master it early on.

In this day and age there are a good number of offerings on the market ranging from "good enough" to very sophisticated software applications. Those of us who have been dealing with the "reach out and touch something" for long enough were among the first ones to embrace this evolving technology with passion. And for a good reason as software alone changed long range shooting in many ways.

But we are talking about WIND here, the elusive variable that to tackle down requires a good dose of art. Even today, the so-called wind-doping, is considered by many to be some sort of obscure art, and for a good reason.

At this point, I guess is important to realize that Wind is always affecting the bullet's drag, the critical aerodynamic parameter that defines how well the bullet "cuts the air." Sometimes, we used to think that headwinds or tailwinds should not to be taken into account. This is a false notion and in the ELR world, this can put you down easily. The bottom line is that Wind affects drag from any direction.

Wind is responsible not only for Windage but also for "Aero Dynamic Jump," a vertical deflection caused by the crosswind component of the surface wind. Therefore, these two main factors call for the best ballistics software to appropriately deal with them.

Since wind is rarely blowing constantly from the same direction and speed, the top ballistics programs offers the capability to work with "multiple wind zones." This feature allows the user to "bracket" the wind into several zones entering wind direction and speed for a certain yardage. I'm not saying this is easy to do, but the experienced wind masters know a trick or two to fill in the right data and get the most out the final fire solution.

The best software packages are less than a fistful, and standing up among them is ColdBore from Patagonia Ballistics. A very accurate and robust program based on a proprietary ballistics engine that has proven itself in the game of ELR for over a decade. It's very interesting to see how ColdBore deals with wind; undoubtedly the proprietary engine is calculating the windage differently than the rest, the usual "Point Mass" solvers that make up 99 percent of the market. Some of the most accomplished shooters have reported that Point Mass-based programs fail their windage predictions with a tendency to increase the necessary windage, while ColdBore is right on the money.

But, just as most software solutions out there are lacking, in regards to crosswind component wind corrections, so is our capability to measure or estimate a wind speed number to plug in.

We need to reconsider some aspects of our shooting that many shooters might consider under control when they first buy a new Kestrel, and that are not really under control. The most obvious and the object of this article is the true wind.

The True Winds
Wind is not a constant, it is a dynamic force. It is not constant in direction or speed and changes both as it moves along the surface of the earth (being channeled through creeks towards flat lands) and being heated by the ground and the sun.

To make matters worse the wind can be totally different in different sections of our bullet flight, due to the topography of the zone, the height at which the bullet is flying, and also the chaotic nature of our earth's clouds, sun and winds. Our nature.

I see many shooters with their hand up high, holding their Kestrel to get "a number" a wind speed, something to work with as a starting point. And this is one more proof about how little shooters, as a group, know about the wind.

The only way to get an accurate wind deviation on our bullet is from the point of impact feedback. This is one of the few real data we will ever have, but in many environments is difficult to see, and is perishable in time. The wind we see affecting our bullet now may not even be there anymore in seconds, no matter how fast we follow up shots.

Always remember that a 10-mph head wind takes over three minutes to get to you from 1000 yards so the wind you feel in the face is the past, not the future. It is not the wind your bullet will be flying in when you shoot it. Now think about a tail wind.

So, if we can't always trust to have a shot's feedback on the *true winds*, and the wind we have at the firing position is not the wind your bullet will fly in. How can we proceed?

How to Proceed

This sets up our first strategic decision we have to make when shooting ELR in the wind. Either we are required to achieve a cold bore shot, or we can live with a first-round miss. There is a strategy for each situation:

1. If we are required to achieve a cold bore shot, we will need to *previously* spend time analyzing the physical characteristics of the ground from our muzzle to the target, and prepare a plan, with multiple variations. Snipers and long-range hunters need such a dynamic plan, which takes into consideration that the wind can change over

time and also takes into account the predicted winds and how these winds will interact with the ground and affect our shooting.

2. Most target shooters that are allowed sighters and those competing ELR with a good target background, can live with a first-round miss. These shooters will also make a plan and may even make custom wind tables for the possible conditions but will seldom spend the amount of effort the first group will. This is because, on many occasions, they will be able to use the best wind estimation available: their impacts.

For the first group you will need to previously find a topo map of the area, or Google Earth image, and a good prediction of the prevalent winds at ground level from any weather agency. If you add an isobaric map and hourly prediction you will also be able to predict how the winds will evolve during the day.

I have prepared a graphic of how I would predict the wind flow on some 2500-yards shots at Monster Lake Ranch in Cody WY, where I am bird hunting while I write this. This FFP (Final Firing Position) allows me to show on a simple-to-understand graphic how the wind would behave and how complex it would be to define its direction and strength just by observation alone.

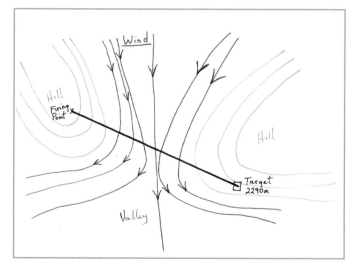

Figure 67. Wind flow on complex terrain

From the FFP you would feel the wind like it's coming from your 11 o'clock or even directly facing you, because you are directly on the area where the wind rotates to the west trying to flow to the valley after coming out the creek. In reality, the wind is only coming "facing" you for a few hundred meters and in reality, is flowing with a nearly crosswind component coming from your 8 o'clock for most of the bullet flight. On the last 300 meters or so, it does shift to a 7 o'clock tailwind for the last section of its flight.

Therefore, you should first measure the different sectors that divide what you predict the wind will do when you shoot. Then estimate the wind velocity using your Kestrel reading at FFP and consider that the central sector of flight will have a more compressed flow and therefore a higher wind velocity.

Applying the same *wind VS terrain* logic, think that wind climbs slopes and mountain sides so the resulting bullet deflection will have a vertical component that might be difficult to estimate. Just the opposite if the wind goes down towards the valley pushing our bullet down.

As you can see, this new *wind reading* takes time and knowledge, so it will take extra time and know-how. Once you have done your pre-shooting work you can jump to the last part of the process which is what the second group do, without the pre-flight complexities we just contemplated.

Cutting Corners

The second group will jump directly to the software input using a ballistics software that can input multiple winds and divide the bullet flight just by observation, in the three sectors. They will then input the wind speed estimate by watching how the wind would flow and comparing it to the wind reading from their Kestrel at the FFP (Final Firing Position). Basically, it's the same thing the first group did, with a lower level of a planning. This group will miss the subtleties of vertical components, turbulences or possible rapid changes, but they will also get a good fire solution that might be good enough.

Either way, we can't do much more now, and using these two approaches, the fire solution will then be as accurate as we, as ELR shooters, can predict with the tools we have today.

Conclusion

Whatever you do and no matter which of the two you decide to apply, if you don't rely on a multi-wind ballistic software or, (worst case scenario) on a single-wind good ballistic solver, you don't stand a chance to get first-round hits at ELR. Forget about paper tables for ELR as your shooting will become frustrating and misses common.

On the other hand, if you eliminate the unknowns by measuring all your shooting parameters, use a multi-wind solver and study the terrain interactions, you will have a lot of fun, enjoy the planning and execution of the shots and feel the *Black Art* of ELR wind shooting. This is not black magic, but a somewhat scientific approach to what many might consider impossible shots.

RICK ASHTON, AUSTRALIA

The first half dozen points you will get from most experts. They are about the basics and being properly prepared. The remaining points are some of the tricks that I guess you are looking for. The basics are the most important. Without them—nothing works.

Think in Terms of Value

The first thing applies to all wind shooting. Think strictly in terms of the value of the wind in points or MOA, but never, never, never think of wind in terms of change or of correction needed. Think, "I need 6 left!" Avoid thinking, "It's up a bit. I'd better go a half more to the left." It's much easier to stay in step if you think in terms of actual values than changes.

Make Sure the Wind Zero Is Correct

The second thing also applies to all wind shooting. Make sure the wind zero on the rifle is correct. There is little satisfaction from getting the wind call right if it's wasted due to a poor zero.

Zeroing is not done by a single visit to the zero range. It takes time and must be done across the range from the shorts to the longs. It's best done with a partner, going shot-for-shot in a variety of conditions, but hopefully around centerline—early morning can be good for this. But make sure that the partner's gun shows similar sight movements as your own, or things won't easily work out. The easiest way to make sure your partner's gun "moves" as your own is to compare elevation differences from the shortest range to the longest range. This one comparison measures directly all the combinations of sight radius, chamber differences, muzzle velocity, load variations, etc.

Make Sure Your Sights Are Square

Make sure the sights are truly square, in a practical sense. This can be done by instruments in a machine shop but then ought to be tested on the range. I advocate setting up a long-range target, but shooting at it from close range, say 100 yards. Scale down the aiming mark to a size you can see best. (The idea here is to take sighting error out of the equation.)

- Fire a five-shot group at centerline at your normal 1,000 yards elevation. Have the marker pull the target, then carefully, using a spirit level, pencil in a perfectly horizontal line through the center of the five-shot group.
- Next, wind out left 25 points; fire five more shots.
- Then set the sight on 25 right and fire five more shots.
- Then return back to the centerline, down to 300-yard elevation, and fire five more shots.

Do not mark the target between shots; just shoot. When you've finished, the left group and right group ought to straddle the horizontal line, and ought to be the same distance from the centerline group. If not, record the differences. Also, if you were to connect the centers of the two groups fired on centerline with a straight line, that line ought to be perfectly square to the horizontal line drawn after the first group.

Why might this not work, even if set up perfectly in a machine shop? One factor is cheek pressure and cheekpiece design—crucial in long range.

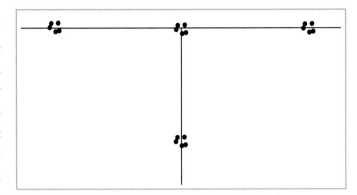

Figure 68. Make sure your sights are square.

Shoot It Square

Having set the rifle up to be square, then shoot it square. I believe a spirit level is essential at long range to eliminate cant and the resultant "Burke's bulges."[2] If the rifle still "wants to cant," then fix (rotate) the buttplate until the rifle's sights are naturally square to the target.

Use a Scorebook

Use a scorebook whenever possible/practicable and use it intelligently. One of the first really good books on shooting I read was the late Des Burke's *Canadian Bisley Shooting*. In it he referred to the practice of "ranging." I think that this is what long-range shooting is all about. We all seek precision, but when it comes to long-range shooting, the route that seems to take us closest is to acknowledge that there is no such thing as precision and to come up with practical tools to help eliminate or reduce bad decisions and help us make good decisions.

Set Up a "Proxy" Wind Flag

When firing in rear fishtail winds, if possible, set up a "proxy" wind flag so that there is a straight line between the proxy flag, through the firing point, in relation to the target in question. The proxy flag might be a team banner erected in just the right spot. It might be a streamer tied to a car aerial.

The tactic is to fire only when the proxy streamer is on the selected side of centerline. This can very much reduce the chances of "getting lost." I reckon this cuts considerably the probability of wind-reading error. You need to be reasonably snappy with the shooting cadence, so as to get the shots downrange when the conditions are right. This also works in angled winds, either rear or frontal, when no "official flag" is directly observable for angle—simply adjust the position of the proxy flag so that it is in line with the mean wind direction and the firing point.

Favor the "Drop-Off"

I reckon that around two-thirds of changes in "fluky" winds are "drop-offs," and one-third are "pick-ups"—therefore, if the wind is coming from the left, set your group in the right-hand sector of the center (or of the bull if it's really tough).

Observe Others' Shots

Use a wide-angled eyepiece if you can. A better change predictor than either flags or mirage is fall of shot. Observe the shots on the range as a whole (or of as much of it as you can see). This is indicative only but can help. It's important to check the squadding on neighboring targets to ensure that the shooters who will share your time slot are worth watching—but don't watch a particular shooter; watch the range.

Use Mirage

Always check mirage—but be careful about how much you factor in its effects. Use a low-power eyepiece (15X), if you can. This will give you a deeper look at mirage; a higher-powered eyepiece might pick up more mirage, but it will tend to be at a localized point on the range.

Put the target in the bottom of the scope's picture at long range. The bullet's trajectory is well above the line of sight—you should be looking high in the scope for the mirage. Do not fire if mirage is "swirling," even if there is no apparent change to the wind flags—a "mystery" wind, elevation, or corner shot may result. Be careful about firing points downrange when reading mirage at long range. Sometimes the only mirage you'll pick up is that on top of a shorter firing point; it will be very localized and may be unrepresentative of what's happening in total. Place low weighting on mirage in frontal fishtails.

Maintain Composure

Maintain as much composure as possible, even in the tough stuff—an inner on the waterline is better than a magpie in the corner.

SERGE BISSONNETTE, CSM, CANADA MEMBER OF DCRA HALL OF FAME

My First Exposure

Just to lighten your day, I will share with you my first exposure to scientific wind calling.

In 1977, I was part of Mike Walker's team to New Zealand (adjutant) and came across a colorful Kiwi from Greymouth named Morley Callahan. Morley was not a big hitter, but during the NZ-NRA Grand, he posted a 49/50 at 1,000 yards, with conditions that only New Zealand's Trentham Range can stir up. He was a clear four points ahead of the second-place shooter, with the average master score being 41/50.

Everyone was asking Morley what was his secret in deciphering the winds. Morley advised that when he was placing his equipment down on the firing point, he split the rear seam on his trousers and did not have the time to change them (knowing Morley, he wouldn't have changed them anyway).

His clear and concise instructions were: "Every time I felt the wind up the tube, I shot."

I don't know the exact tear size, but it does give credence to mother's advice on wearing clean underwear.

Wind-Judging Drill

1. Show up behind the firing point and do the pre-shoot analysis:
   A. Look at the lay of the land to see if there are evident features that may contribute to or interfere with the consistent flow of air, such as a tree line ("A" Range,

Connaught), a hill (Homestead Range, Calgary), or a ravine (St. Bruno Range, Quebec).

B. Look for patterns of air flow; compare wind flag pitch and angle with the mirage.

C. Check wind chart for parameters when there is a strong condition and when there is a mild condition. If stable, the job is easier.

2. Take up the shooting position:

A. Lift head and feel the breeze; most times it's different than when you're standing or sitting.

B. Confirm pattern; look at grass for low movement and flags for high movement.

C. Note angle and mark on "call" section of plot sheet.

D. Scope the mirage; off-focus target, about 100 meters front of target.

E. Mark the SWAG, your best "scientific wild-ass guess," on your plot sheet; and sight which should be in line with your wind chart.

3. Fire the shot:

A. Sight alignment—confirm "feel" and flag.

B. Sight picture—confirm "feel" and mirage.

C. Execute the shot; focus word; follow through; call shot; mark my call.

D. Confirm conditions—flag and mirage.

4. After the signal, do the following:

A. Graph—compare graph setting to wind chart for difference. This is to have a reference in case of a big change. If you rely only on your wind chart and do not calculate the "error factor" on this particular shoot/range, it costs you points to reconfirm a known.

B. Adjust—return to 2(A).

BERT BOWDEN, AUSTRALIA
WINNER OF THE QUEEN'S PRIZE,
AUSTRALIA (THREE TIMES)
PALMA TEAM CAPTAIN (1999, 2003)

In selecting our coaches for Bloemfontein 1999, we would ask aspirants two questions:

1. What wind do you think is on now?

2. How did you work that out?

Responses to the second question caused shudders. Nobody did it in a consistent way—because they'd never been taught, but rather "picked it up" or worked on "gut feel." Our current PALMA team is now training juniors as our future coaches.

[Authors' note: Bert kindly sent us his entire wind-reading lesson plan, which covers the topic most thoroughly. The following shows that we have shamelessly stolen the best, and abbreviated the rest.]

Before we get on to wind reading, I must emphasize that there are some very important elements of preparation that are absolutely critical to good shooting. But more important, they form the basis for becoming confident at reading wind. They are:

• Make sure your rifle is properly zeroed and that the sights are shooting square by shooting a plumb line.

• Make sure your plotting and sight setting are perfectly accurate and that you analyze every shoot immediately afterwards.

• Make sure you can shoot the smallest possible group and that your group is in the middle of the target.

There are four ways of attacking this difficult, but mostly conquerable, thing called wind. The shooter may be able to use one of these approaches throughout a shoot, but on occasion it may be necessary to change approach mid-shoot. It is one thing to start with a plan, but be ready to change to another plan if the conditions dictate. The four approaches are:

• Shoot fast, correcting on the last spotter.

• Treat every shot as a sighter.

• Select a single acceptable condition.

• Play the percentages.

Shoot Fast, Correcting on the Last Spotter

In difficult conditions, *do not* use this method. This method is best suited when conditions are steady or when winds are changing evenly or slowly.

You will often hear it said on the range during extremely bad conditions that the only answer is to shoot fast, correct on the spotter, and beat the changes. This is fraught with danger and a recipe for embarrassment. Don't do it!

The fact is that conditions can change quickly, and even much more quickly than you can shoot. What happens is that you finish up "chasing" yourself all over the target, correcting on bad shots, and suddenly you find yourself neck-deep in trouble.

Treat Every Shot as a Sighter

This method is best suited for the following:

- When conditions are difficult, and an appraisal before every shot is necessary
- When "surprise" conditions are apt to occur
- When shooting two or three to a target (Bisley style)

For those who are confident wind readers, this is where they put their trust. In difficult conditions, a confident wind reader will calculate the setting required, get ready, take aim, check again before firing, and if correct, fire quickly. The essence of this approach is in firing quickly, but only after you are sure of the wind setting.

The one time when this method becomes mandatory is under conditions such as those experienced at Bisley, where there are two or three to shoot on the same target. There, it is most essential to follow the changes in the wind, sometimes making alterations while the other two are firing a shot each, just to keep in touch with any changes.

The one thing that becomes apparent here is that you will always know in terms of how many points (minutes) or windage you have set on the sight. Never, ever, get into the habit of saying that "it's up a bit" or "it's down a bit." That's not wind reading; that is trying to guess the differences!

Select a Single Acceptable Condition

A recurring condition is one that you expect to keep occurring, and, if you intend to use this method, you must choose a condition that is expected to occur most often. There is no point in selecting a condition that will happen only once every 10 minutes and be there for, say, 30 seconds. What you want is a condition that will be there for the majority of the time, and preferably stay for the longest period.

This method is best suited to the lapsed-time method of shooting [such as in smallbore matches and in ISSF 300-meter matches].

A recurring condition might be a flag in line with a pole, a flag on one side or the other of a pole, or any flag that shows a constant condition.

Play the Percentages

With this method, it is usually as a result of observation of the conditions before you shoot. You should get into the habit of always observing before you shoot. For at least 15 minutes before your turn to take the mound, you should preferably sit behind a line of flags, with your telescope firmly in hand, and check the variations in mirage and flags. During this time you can determine what sort of approach you will take, based on your observations.

If you decide to play the percentages, what you have observed is that all the changes (if there are any) are not enough to put you out of the bull. For example, there may be a steady 3-point crosswind which occasionally flicks up to about 4, but that's all. On that basis, with your sight set on 3½ points, you could comfortably shoot at your own pace and expect the group to wander from one side of the bull to the other.

You must always check, though, before you fire every shot. Remember that wind is fickle, and the one you don't check before firing is the one that will get away on you.

Three General Statements

1. A shooter who fires a shot without being sure is letting the conditions master him. Strive always to be master over the conditions!

2. Everyone starts each competition equal (that is, with the possible number of points). Throw nothing away.

3. Everyone makes mistakes. Strive to make fewer mistakes than your opposition.[3] If you make a mistake, always work out why and strive never to repeat it!

The Bowden Method

A flag will always show an "approximate" condition. It is nearly impossible to judge exactly from any flag, and you will notice if you read up on findings from studies of wind effect in shooting, that there's almost a sixth sense required that tells you the calculation should be just a touch more or just a touch less. So, out of it all we learn to read an "approximation" in the flags until it becomes second nature to us.

Wind speed	Speed factor	Distance				
		800 y	800 m	900 y	900 m	1000 y
		Distance multiplier				
		7	8	9	10	10
20 mph	2	= 2 x 7	= 2 x 8	= 2 x 9	= 2 x 10	= 2 x 10
16 mph	1½	= 1½ x 7	= 1½ x 8	= 1½ x 9	= 1½ x 10	= 1½ x 10
12 mph	1	= 1 x 7	= 1 x 8	= 1 x 9	= 1 x 10	= 1 x 10
8 mph	½	= ½ x 7	= ½ x 8	= ½ x 9	= ½ x 10	= ½ x 10
4 mph	¼	= ¼ x 7	= ¼ x 8	= ¼ x 9	= ¼ x 10	= ¼ x 10

Figure 69. Speed factor chart.

Wind direction	12:30	1:00	1:30	2:00	3:00
Direction factor	¼	½	⁷⁄₁₀	⅞	1

Figure 70. Direction factor chart.

In his book *Competitive Rifle Shooting*, Jim Sweet recommends a comprehensive table of estimating wind shown on the flags in mph. Employing the KISS principle,

I use a variation of a method that Clive Halnan has written about. The wind speed is read from the position of the flag tip, and the speed factor is applied to the distance multiplier. In effect, the shooter need only memorize the speed factor and the distance multiplier in order to calculate the wind settings.

These are effectively the 3 o'clock and 9 o'clock sight settings for all distances. Let's go on with direction allowances. There are four additional figures to be used as direction factors, and with thanks to Jim Sweet, here they are shown in Figure 70.

Mirage

First, what is mirage? To you, the shooter, mirage is wind that you can see through your telescope. To those who study atmospherics, it is the result of the disturbance of air, layers of different temperature, or eddies. To me, mirage is a most important aid to your shooting. It is also the prime reason for owning a good telescope, 25-power or better.

Here are some basic points about mirage:

- It can't be seen when light is dull.
- It is of no use for winds over 8 mph (13 kph).
- It can be a trap in varying light.
- It can change in either strength or direction.
- It can be used to complement or confirm flag readings.

How do you see mirage in the first place? Basically, focus your telescope on the target. Then defocus toward you. That is, focus on an imaginary point between you and the target. What I do is focus on an object about one-third of the distance down-range. (For example, if I am shooting at 900 yards, I focus on something at 600 yards.) Then I swing the scope back onto the target. I've found that this approach gives me a consistent way of getting mirage pictures at the point in flight where the wind effect is most relevant. This way, I see (at a particular distance) what I usually see.

Figure 71. Mirage factor chart.

Mirage description	Wind speed	Mirage factor
Boiling	Zero wind	0
		¼
Drifting	Up to 4 mph	½
		¾
Flowing	Between 4-8 mph	1
Running	8 mph and over	Flag

There are four basic stages of mirage, listed in Figure 71. Mirage factors can be applied to the distance multiplier the same way that speed factors were applied earlier.

If mirage is present, check it before every shot. Position the eyepiece of your telescope so that you can check mirage without having to move from your firing position to do so.

Other Wind Factors

I want to emphasize that the wind allowances that I've mentioned are based on having all flags along the range indicating the same thing. Those of you who have been flag-watching will already know that this is a rare phenomenon. More often than not, no two flags show the same strength and/or direction. In some cases, they can show wind from both sides at the same time, as happens on some of the more infamous ranges like Canberra's McIntosh Range.

When you run into this situation, you have three choices:

- Ignore it, do nothing, shoot again.
- Take a guess, do something or nothing, shoot again.
- Calculate it as near as possible.

What do you think is the preferred thing to do? Right: calculate it as near as possible. Remember, wind reading is about knowing; guessing has no place.

General Tips
- Always calculate, never guess.
- Develop your shooting rhythm to aid wind reading.

- The shot on the left or right is not necessarily because of a wind change.
- If it's raining, the flags will probably be wet; be aware that they won't show the full allowance.
- Rain is like a wet mirage. The angle at which it is falling can be an aid to wind reading. Check through your telescope.
- If you are having trouble with the wind, so are most of the other shooters.
- Don't "creep." If the conditions have changed and you've calculated a move, have the confidence to move the sight accordingly.
- It's best to use a flag that's showing wind coming toward you, rather than one showing what's already gone.
- God planted trees and grass to aid shooters. Use them to detect when gusts and other inconsistent conditions are occurring.
- Never fire in the middle of an obvious change (or gust). Wait for conditions to settle, if match conditions allow. Use the rules to advantage; challenge your last shot if you need to gain more time.
- Never move on another shooter's spotter. He's more likely to pull wild shots than you are.
- If confusion sets in, stop and recalculate.
- That last, quick check of the flags before releasing the shot is worth its weight in Queen's badges.
- More possibles are made with steady, deliberate shooting than with hurried panic.

DON BROOK, AUSTRALIA

Why This Is a Difficult Question

I was asked to coach the army Under-25 team in New Zealand, at 1,000 yards, and when I questioned the two top army wind coaches about what they thought the wind was doing and how much was on, I was presented with "I'm blowed if I know." So, we split it three ways: one went with 32 right, the other with 28, and I went with 24. Thirty-two produced a dead-center bull, while the rest of us missed it!

When I asked what he had done to work this out, his curt reply was "I really do not know; it just looked like 32."

How can you promulgate that sort of reply?

So I know what you are up against. There are so many wind readers out there who just rely on a millennium of experience, but cannot write or teach it.

In my case, I have had access to the finest smallbore shooters in the world, blokes who can explain, and I have learned heaps from Ernie Van De Zande and Lones Wigger Jr., and then worked very closely with one of the best sports psychologists I have ever seen in how to approach the wind problems within the mind and make a decision based on the facts that confront the shooter.

I can relate one instance when I fired a prone 60 shots in Linz in Austria, in the most horrific wind conditions I have ever fired a smallbore match. Ernie Van De Zande fired a 600, which absolutely astounded me, while my own score, a 592 (with a 100 in the final string), ran second. Ernie and I spoke for five hours over this, and when I could get back to my hotel, I wrote it all down. That bloke fired that match in absolute genius mode, and we were the only two shooters over 590 points.

A Story About Where Wind Knowledge Helped Me

I am not sure what you want, apart from some instances where wind knowledge helped me. With this in mind, here is one you may be able to use that happened to me a long time ago, in the days of my .303 rifle.

I was in a big shoot-off for an 800-yard match in the 1969 NSW Queens. Forty-two other blokes and I all had 15 bull possibles! We all lined up on the mound with the flags hanging dead down the poles in the pre-calm of an approaching southerly storm on Anzac range in Sydney. This storm looked really ugly coming in, and my pre-match thinking was to get my shots down the range about 10 feet

apart! We started, and I fired two sighters, both in, and three bulls pretty quickly, when the wind hit, and how! Poles were bending with the flags looking like they were starched. Just as the wind hit us, a shooter on my right, who ultimately went on to win the Queens, fired his second shot. I was wondering just how many points were required in this enormously strong storm, when *my* target went down and was marked an outer, on the very edge of the board at three o'clock. I told him he had shot on my plate and was met with a curt reply, "Bulldust."

So, here I was thinking perhaps 35 points in the change, when it hit me . . . I altered my sight five points left, aimed at his target, and hit mine smack in the middle! I shot the only possible on the range, with the last two shots aimed on my friend's target on the right, with five points left on the wind arm, won the match and 25 quid for my thinking.

I was pretty chuffed with that!

On the Virtues of Aiming Off and Shading

The fastest way to combat wind deviation is using the aiming-off and shading-the-aim routine.

Aiming off is "big increment" stuff, to even off the target. Lining up the side of the target with the exterior edge of the ring gives you about 10 minutes of angle, depending on the range being fired. Obviously, edge sighting at 300 is a heap different to 1,000 in terms of minutes.

Shading the aim is very fine increments, even to nominating a shot within the V-ring, and largely this type is positive thought, induced by command to the subconscious mind.

I found, in smallbore aiming, that with training I could aim so accurately with this, I could nominate a 10.1 at clock rotation, and shoot out the bull in 12 shots going around the clock. I can aim within the 10-ring anywhere I want to put the shot, and this is very valuable wind combat stuff. Does this lot scare you?

To be fair, I do not know of any elite-level smallbore shooter who cannot do this, and many utilize the bubble cant as well as a wind combat method.

These are just more tools in the bag of tricks. Lately, I have been perfecting techniques with the electronic computer systems, and these really sharpen up the aiming process.

More on Aiming Off and Shading

Teaching this to the army squad created an enormous amount of controversy, as nearly all the fullbore shooters I have come into contact with are reticent to adjusting the aim away from dead center. Smallbore shooters and elite-level 300-meter shooters are way ahead in this area.

We have a range in Australia (Canberra, where the National Queens is staged every year) that is extremely fast in wind variations, both in increase and decrease, plus direction changes. Mirage also overrides any small variations. This range can be very difficult, and introduces a psychological barrier as well. Mostly the shooters get carved up in a big way because of their inflexibility of aiming.

I taught our army squad to circumvent this by the psychological attitude that they are the boss. The rifle will never shoot Vs while it stands in a corner, eh? In order to teach this, obviously [I had to do] a lot of groundwork in wind reading, particularly in Canberra, where the range slopes sideways about 10 degrees to the right. This alters the plane of wind effect from normal, to be roughly parallel with the ground.

In learning to shade, or aim off either uphill or down, they have to have the confidence to try this method. The rifles need to be zeroed exactly (as should be the case anyway). Most of my squad had a tough time in gaining the control to muscle the rifle slightly, to effect the required aim, but soon got over the problem when the central bulls arrived. Funny, that!

To outline the thought process for you requires a scenario for you to imagine. I often shoot on another range in Australia (Mudgee) where the sighting in the morning is as crisp as glass, and I was down early with the early-morning wind at half value. After getting the wind zero directly into the central at 10 o'clock, as I maintained the wind would increase rather than drop off (I was correct). I proceeded to aim where I wanted to in the method of combat upwind. In other words, showing a full bull in the aim toward 10 o'clock in the ring sight. (The aiming mark was at 4 o'clock.) I try to visualize a fine set of crosshairs, so I can be really accurate where I put the aim. As the shoot progressed, I needed to sharpen the wind assessment in value and vary the aiming accordingly, so the continual judgment was as clinical as I could put together.

The shoot flowed along very quickly, as it happened, and I was off the mound, with a match-winning 50.9 in 6 minutes. One of my club mates mentioned to my wife, Cheryl, who was watching: "Look at that, he shot right through then without touching the sights. What a lucky patch!" I didn't tell him I was shading the aim, on at least six of the ten shots.

As a footnote, the club mate went down later and tried to battle the wind variations. He was slow and wound up with a 48.3.

The method works, but you have to have the courage of your own convictions with reading the wind, analyzing what is out there, and using the combat method you decide on. The thought processes I employ are very clinical in assessment, and I will often move the sight back to wind zero, and make my own new adjustment, on the value that I think is out there based on many and tried observation techniques . . . assessment of direction in the half-value winds, flag ripple speeds, and tip elevation in full-value winds. This is not just an accident of years of learning; it is a very exact science. There are mathematical geniuses in our sport who quickly assess the values using cosine and even trig to arrive at the assessments.

JIM BULLOCK, G.C., CANADA
MEMBER OF DCRA HALL OF FAME

A River of Wind

More than once I have seen wind flags pointing at each other. The wind is *not* an even flow of air like the water in a slow, wide river. As our bullet goes downrange it passes through patches of air moving at different speeds and at different angles. The displacement we see on the target is the *average* result of all those influences.

Each few seconds, the effect of the wind influence changes. Have you ever finished a match in which you struggled with the wind, while the cadet beside you shot well and proclaimed, "I never touched my sight!"? The wind keeps changing, and for one shooter it can change back to the same condition each time it is his turn to shoot.

Let's consider wind strategy in several steps.

Before the Match

Arrive early, pull out your Parker Hale whiz wheel, and follow the wind for a while. The flags will give you a feel for the approximate average direction and strength and a feel for the magnitude and frequency of changes. The wheel will give you a feel for the number of minutes associated with a change of direction or strength. This helps you mentally "change gears" as you move from one distance to another. At 600 yards I would say to myself, "Okay, if I see a change, it is at least a one-minute change."

As shooters leave the mound, ask them, "How did it go?" Some will give you a detailed explanation of the key flags, the wind shifts, and magnitudes of change. Look at their plots, if possible.

During the Match

Mirage is the best indicator of wind. Focus your scope on a mound 100 or 200 yards in front of you. If mirage cannot be used, the best flags are the ones close to you

and upwind. Another excellent wind indicator is the shots of other competitors. If you see a number of downwind inners and magpies, you know there was a shift that caught them.

If the conditions are changing frequently, a Plot-o-Matic (EZ-Graf) quickly shows the extremes of the changes. I find it easy to write in a little arrow, showing flag angle, and a little picture of the flag to show strength, beside each shot number. If the wind fishtails, the zero sight setting will be between two flag pictures showing the wind going in opposite directions. If there is a major change, you have a pictorial reference as to wind strength and angle to refer to. This is very handy if you have to come back to a condition that occurred much earlier in the match.

I once struggled at long range, making major changes, only to find that I had two settings on the rifle—too much and not enough. After the match I looked at George Chase's Plot-o-Matic (EZ-Graf). It was obvious that although the wind kept changing, it was changing from a strong right wind to a mild right wind, and that if I had shot the match with 11 minutes or 4 minutes, a possible was there to be had. George almost had the possible, because he quickly recognized that there were only the two mean wind conditions. I was so busy reading the wind I did not catch on to the reality.

Shooting is a game of averages. There is an average wind, made up of strong and mild components. There is an average group, made up of an extreme left and extreme right aiming and ammo component. It is a mathematical certainty that the best score will occur when the group is centered over the bull. Even if you miss a wind change, there is a good chance of a bull if the group is centered. If it is a quarter-minute high or low, the bull is much smaller. If you find yourself thinking, "The last four shots are a bit high—if this one is high, I will come down a quarter," then you are probably not being as diligent as you should be with your group centering. Centering the group makes the bull bigger.

There are other wind indicators that can be used in some conditions:

- On a very, very light wind day, especially if there is a fishtail condition, the muzzle smoke indicates which way the wind is going. This is handy when there is no mirage.
- Tossing a tuft of grass in the air can show a light wind direction.
- A lot of inners out the same side of the target is a sure sign something happened.
- Watch your shooting partner's shots. An upwind or downwind inner may be a perfect indicator of direction and magnitude of a wind change. (Or it may mean a bad shot. Check other targets.)

Wind Reading

An understanding of wind is necessary in order to develop a strategy to handle it. I started this article by saying, "As our bullet goes downrange it passes through patches of air moving at different speeds and at different angles. The displacement we see on the target is the average result of all those influences."

At long range, we must take into account the air mass passing through a large box of air in front of us. A gust of wind on our cheek may be quite irrelevant, given all the air in front of us. One of the assets we have to work with is a few seconds of time allocated for the shot. Assuming you can see several flags, make it a rule not to shoot until all the flags are going the same direction. The angle may vary between flags, but don't shoot until the box of air in front of you (or the box of air moving toward you from the upwind flags) is all moving in the same direction. If you shoot in a swirl condition, it is a temporary condition that is difficult to read and even more difficult to record for future reference. In practice, this means that most of your shots will be fired quickly, and occasionally you will need to use most of your 45 seconds to let the wind stabilize.

After the Match

We all have some ability to see a wind change and then say, "That's a two-minute increase," and then take the shot. After each match it is useful to do a postmortem and analyze how accurately we made the wind changes. One thing I do is note the times I made a wind change based on an observed wind change (as opposed to a group-centering adjustment) and mark the change with a + or a - depending on whether I over- or under-adjusted. If I have a lot more minus marks than I have plus marks, then I know I am being too tentative in my changes. If you tend to over-adjust at short range and under-adjust at long range, this little exercise will quickly expose the problem. I also mark with a ? when I have made a change that seemed uncalled for. A lot of question marks means I am trying too hard and seeing changes that are not there.

GEORGE CHASE, CANADA
MEMBER OF DCRA HALL OF FAME

What you are about to receive from shooters around the world should make for an interesting read. The mind-set of American shooters, with their style of string shooting, should be very different from the pairs, and even three to a target, of the English. With the world becoming so small, with the use of computers and the group sizes following the same course, I will look forward to the final production of your wind book. Yes, it will make an interesting read.

Lights started going on for me when I began using a plotting board. I was a poor recorder of useful information using the plot and graphs. The board began to show me how few changes there really were on the range. It showed me the difference between wind and mistakes, and constantly told me to center my group; with the true picture I became more comfortable and confident. With confidence came smaller groups.

In a conversation with one of Canada's better shooters I asked the question, "How would you go about picking a wind coach?" and without hesitation he replied, "If we had access to everyone's plotting cards and we knew they were honest, I would simply choose the shooter with the biggest groups and highest scores." World-class shooters shoot small groups. Great wind coaches are, for the most part, made that way by great shooters and great conditions. I'm sure within the pages of your book you will answer questions on all aspects of the wind. Those who can cope with all their minds can cram in and make a decision on what to do while shooting a small group will be the winners at the end of the day.

Your plotting board or sheet should be your greatest aid in reading varying conditions. Being able to return to the same sight setting for a similar condition is not something for which you should rely on memory or a best guess. Plot as accurately as possible and you will be amazed how the range settles down.

I think it's impossible to separate wind reading and group formation. When the wind is switching from 7 right to 7 left, shooters are going to come away with poor scores. There are some that may pooh-pooh a 5- or 10-minute change, but scores will fall. It's when the changes are gentle that we must be aware of all our little mistakes that we attribute to wind; these hurt our scores. Sometimes we are looking for wind that is not there. In the pre-F-Class days, I was shooting with one of the finest gunsmiths in North America; you knew he had the finest equipment available. We were at 800 meters, and his score was not impressive for the conditions. The very next year, same match, close to the same conditions, he shot a 50 with 10 Vs. Did he have a bad shoot the year before? No, he shot his average score. Did he, in one year, learn all the deep dark secrets of wind reading? No; what he did with the aid of a scope was to stop chasing sighting errors.

I know the greatest evaluation of what's happening on the range is the shot placement on the targets. Read the targets, at least six, quickly evaluate the center of mass, make your change, and shoot.

STUART COLLINGS, GREAT BRITAIN

I have always thought that wind reading is a black art and that most coaches don't really know exactly how they do it. Sometimes they are in tune with it, and sometimes they aren't. It depends, among other things, on their mood, time of the month, the type of wind that day, and, of course, the quality of the shooter. As far as tips and pointers go, I can think of a few.

- At long range, think of the wind as a body of air moving across the range from muzzle to target. I don't subscribe to the view that wind at the firing point end is necessarily more important than wind at the target end.
- Judge an absolute value for the wind for each shot rather than going purely on an estimate of how much it has changed since the previous one.
- Get a fix on speed and angle on an upwind row of flags running down the range, and after the decision get the shot away with the same rhythm each time. If the nearest row of upwind flags is 10 targets away, the rhythm may be slower. If it is just alongside, you need to get it off quickly. Bear in mind, though, that the wind can sometimes billow down from above along a broad front and can lift several flags across the range at the same time. Also, if there are only a few flags down the range, then a gust can zip through between them. Tricky, eh!
- Don't always believe fall of shot on your target. Be confident of your calls.
- Team wind coaching is a team effort. Use information from your other targets constantly.
- If flags and mirage disagree—stop.

KEITH CUNNINGHAM, CANADA
MEMBER OF DCRA HALL OF FAME

For most of my shooting career, I have never had a plan about reading the wind. I tried to get information from other shooters before I went up on the line, studied charts (guessing at wind speeds), and from then on it was more of a reactionary shoot.

It wasn't until I went to the World Long Range Championships in South Africa in 1999 that I actually went onto the line with a plan. I knew what the bookends would be and which flag(s) I was going to watch. I knew whether this was going to be a direction shoot or a wind speed shoot.

I like to arrive at my firing point at least a half hour before I am to shoot. I now use a wind meter, which tells me at what speed the wind is really traveling. For years I would go out and look at a flag and only guess at the speed; not ever having actually seen a flag that I knew was flying at 10 kph, it was impossible to say for sure that this flag looks like 10 kph. With the wind meter, I can now learn to recognize wind speed much more accurately. One is not allowed to use the wind meter on the firing line during a shoot, but during my preliminary study I memorize the flag condition as it relates to the wind meter reading, so that I can recognize this condition as the primary one and relate it to other conditions if I have to shoot in the changes.

Once I have studied the wind direction and speed for a while, I refer to a set of charts, which I find are simple and easy to read, for my initial setting. Linda and I came up with these charts and teach them on our police sniper courses. I wanted to provide the police with something that minimized the number of pages they had to carry around, and was straightforward and simple to read. I have always found that these charts will, at least, keep me in the inner and near the bull, with my opening shot.

I fire my sighting shots as carefully as any of the other shots. These shots are not "just sighters," but shots from which I am going to get a more accurate reading of what the wind is really doing in this condition. I memorize the flags, both for speed and direction, and now know what should be on the sight for that condition. I use a Plot-o-Matic (EZ-Graf) to plot my shots, and as long as the wind stays in my memorized condition, I know what I should have on the sight.

For each shot I go through a little "ask the question" game to help me come to a decision about what the sight should be at for the next shot:

"Is the wind the same or different?"

If it is the same, I carry on with what I know.

If it is different, I ask another question: "Has its value increased or decreased?" This will tell me what direction I am going to change the sight. Then:

"Has it changed a little or a lot?" This will get me mentally prepared to make the correct amount of change. I then refer to my plot to see what the bookends have been and decide if this condition is outside or inside those bookends. I also have a look at the other targets to see what the average error is on those targets, to get a feel as to how much I should change. I then make a decision, set my sights to the specific windage, and fire my next shot.

One point that seems to help: after each shot I see where my shot landed and immediately make a sight correction to center that shot. To help calibrate my thinking, I say to myself, for example, "Okay, that's the wind condition that needs 2 minutes left." And then I decide what my next sight setting will be from where the sight is now set. This reestablishes my baseline position and helps to keep my group centered.

To summarize: find out quickly what you need to have on the sight for a certain condition, memorize the flags or mirage appearance for that condition, and make future decisions from that known point.

CLINT DAHLSTROM, CANADA

To shoot a long-range bull's-eye, the shooter has to do three things very well:

1. Previous shots must be analyzed to coordinate wind judgment with the realities of the day and the range.

2. With that calibration of judgment, observations of current conditions must be converted to sight settings.

3. Then a perfect shot must follow that sight adjustment very, very quickly.

Every shooter has a personal procedure for executing each step, and that is just as it should be. The critical thing is that these must not be three separate activities—they must be part of a single, integrated whole.

The shooter must have a standard program that naturally progresses step-by-step, without omission, from recording the last shot to firing the next. The shooter's mind-set has to be such that a typical step description goes like this: "Immediately after clicking on the wind, I always center my target number in the aperture and then come down (or up) to center my bull in a perfect sight picture." It is critical that the attitude be such that the word "always" pops out naturally, in describing the transitions from analysis to wind decision to shot release, because those transitions are the weak link in most programs—where momentary inattention or other poor execution may allow errors such as missing a wind change or shooting a V on the target next door.

Additional Words of Wisdom from Clint Dahlstrom[4]

The following advice is intended for folks who think they can substitute wind judging for good "holding and squeezing."

It is easy to say that one needs an efficient personal system, but developing it takes a lot of time and dedicated effort. For those lucky enough to have a mentor, such as a parent in a shooting family or a dedicated coach in a local club, the task is easier (but still not easy). However, many of the very best attained that status without the advantage of mentor assistance. A common, and quite practical, program is to start by rather slavishly imitating the masters. Without being overly intrusive, one can learn from them effective procedures with which to build a basic program

by observing and talking and reading. After substantial progress, perhaps to mid-master level, one may begin to suspect that, while the basic principles are surely valid, some of the procedures employed by the very best are "individual-specific prescriptions." Optimal shooting programs are not a one-size-fits-all proposition, because people differ in physical and mental attributes. The next stage, then, is to identify and incorporate those modifications that will aid in delivering the very best shots that one can fire.

As a simple example, consider ISSF prone shooting at 50 or 300 meters where many (most?) of the elite use "shading" or "holding over" techniques in coping with certain wind conditions. Confidently effective use of these techniques requires the crisp, clear sight picture provided by excellent visual acuity, and fully functional focal accommodation. Those with imperfect visual acuity, and/or at an age when focal accommodation deteriorates, usually see a fairly clear aperture and a fuzzy bull. This is not optimal (acceptable?) for holding over. However, these are not definitively hopeless conditions. One must simply find another way.

By itself, the primary stage of fully understanding and carefully applying the basic principles of marksmanship will produce a much better than average competitor. In going beyond that stage, the devil is in the details of analyzing one's physical and mental attributes and developing accommodations, within the basic principles, that will optimize personal performance. This is a critical stage. Make no mistake—one cannot hope to be a long-range winner without developing the "holding and squeezing" skills necessary to be a consistent short-range contender and frequent winner. Developing an effective wind-coping system is part of the third-stage graduate course that permits one to benefit from superior marksmanship. It is an essential supporting function. It is not a substitute for flawless shot delivery.

All the champions you admire and hope to emulate have been successful in their personal multistage development campaigns. Those with a talent for teaching do remember the struggles needed to attain the competence they now enjoy. These folks can and will help. Others have abandoned the memories of their development struggles as excess mental baggage and have allowed their subsequent successes to convince them that their current procedures are the universal "right way." This conviction is something for students to cope with now and to remember when they have earned the right to pontificate.

It is easy to lose a competition by inadequate performance in the early simple stages. To win, one must stay with the best in the early stages and then excel in the difficult stages. In multi-range prone rifle matches, the long range is the definitively difficult stage, and usually it is wind judging that determines the winner. To be a consistent winner, you must put a very high priority, and a hell of a lot of dedication, into developing your own best possible system for shot delivery and wind coping.

DARREN ENSLIN, ZIMBABWE AND AUSTRALIA INDIVIDUAL WORLD LONG-RANGE RIFLE CHAMPION (1999)

I have been thinking a lot about your book. It certainly is a book on its own due to the complexities of "weather" on a projectile. I am just going to write from my head on the subject. I may sway from things you may want to hear (i.e., common knowledge), but it will be easier for me, and then you can take out and use the bits you want.

I totally agree that weather reading is a learned/subconscious action that tends to get better with time, practice, and confidence on a particular range.

Weather reading (for me) comes in three thinking phases:

1. Shooting a string (single shooter)
2. Shooting in pairs or threes
3. Coaching a shootist

Shooting a String (Single Shooter)

When I shoot by myself in a string shoot (not being coached), I feel my most relaxed. I know that if I shoot fast, which I have the confident ability to do, then I can keep up with the weather and follow shots, and be able to trust that 3 or 9 o'clock shots are weather patterns.

Changing on What I Call the "Future Wind"

I call it this because a lot of people look at the line of flags very close to themselves. By the time you've adjusted for the "present" weather close to you, aimed, and pulled the trigger, it has blown away, and the weather affecting the flags two to three ranges across (the "future") is now with you.

This method contributed to my successful performance at the World Individual Long Range Championships in Bloemfontein. There, the strength in the wind was very much affected by (what I observed to be) flag angle changing two to three ranges across. And I soon learned that there was a pattern in a flag beginning to jump to a new position a few seconds before it actually rested in that new position.

Shooting in Pairs or Threes

Shooting in pairs or threes certainly demands experience and good short-term memory.

You need firstly to guess the weather. Shoot to confirm your guess, then adjust on your guess for the next shot, at the same time considering what the set of flags and mirage looked like, and whether you read the weather correctly or incorrectly for that particular shot. For the start of the shoot, it's more difficult; toward the middle and end of the shoot, one gets more confident with the short-term memory of the weather condition.

What I "think" while shooting/watching the flag is this: once I've established the correct wind strength with sighters, I give that particular flag angle/strength a name; for example, "That's a 3-minute right flag," etc. So when it's your turn to shoot again you have to try and remember which short-term imprinted picture of the flags best suits the next shot.

Coaching

This to me is fairly close to my own string-shooting method, except you've got the whole picture (not having to aim and shoot and miss some of the changes). In Africa, there is normally a lot of mirage that accompanies the wind, and the wind effect on the mirage is normally easy to follow. When the wind blows the mirage slowly, I give the picture the name "Thick Syrup Number X"—the X being the number of minutes required to hit the center. When the wind blows the mirage stronger, then I call the picture "Sugar Water Number X." I'm sure you know why I give the two variables their descriptive names.

For New Shooters

The one thing I wish I had been given the opportunity to do when I first started to shoot was to move the sights into and out of the wind a minute at a time, deliberately moving toward the outer edges of the target to learn how important bold moves are, especially at long range. New shooters are often afraid to move their sights, thinking, "They've been zeroed on the bull. Now leave them." It's often tough to get a new shooter to learn quickly the effect of wind from 300, 500, 600 meters to 700, 800, 900 meters.

ALAIN MARION, CANADA
WINNER OF THE QUEEN'S PRIZE
AT BISLEY (THREE TIMES)
MEMBER OF DCRA HALL OF FAME

To begin with, in most cases wind is an overrated factor. It is an easy excuse for bad holding. If you looked at it closely, you would find that your best wind dopers are the same people who win matches when there is no wind. How many people do you know became wind-judging experts when they changed to F-Class? You have to fire good shots so that you get some benefit from them in order to judge the wind for the next one.

Authors: *When you first arrive at the range for a match, what do you look at and what do you think about?*
AM: What I look at when I get to a match depends on whether I know the range or not. If not, I will study the physical geography of the range to see if a hill, a coulee, or anything else could have an effect on the wind currents.

After that, I watch the wind cycles (sometimes . . . ?), but I try to go into the match without a preconceived idea about what it will do.

Authors: *When you are preparing to set your sight for that first sighter, what do you think about in order to make that decision?*
AM: I take an educated guess for the correction I use for the first sighter; but for a less experienced shooter, it is a good idea to have a wind chart to get started on.

Authors: *When you have the results from your first sighter, what do you think about in order to set your sight for the second sighter?*
AM: For the second sighter, if I think the wind is the same, I correct to three-quarters of a minute of perfect wind. If it is inside that, I leave it alone.

One thing I have found that has helped me is to spot one flag that is coming in my direction for wind angle and another one with its tip in line with something (for example, the top of a line of trees or the hills across the river at Connaught), which gives me an indication of the variations in strength.

In very light wind, I pay a lot of attention to mirage.

By the way, if a shooter misses small wind changes more often than he thinks he should, he might benefit by installing a spirit level on his front sight.

Under all types of conditions, I always watch to see where people are hitting on the targets that are in the field of view of my scope. This method is particularly good in the big finals, as you are surrounded by good shooters.

If there is a very big wind change, I start over as if I were shooting my first sighter. It is easier to get yourself to think "this is 12 minutes left wind" than to think "I need to make a 6-minute correction."

The best words of wisdom I could give a new shooter would be to learn to shoot tight groups and to center them. The rest will follow accordingly.

Additional Words of Wisdom from Alain Marion About Gilmour Boa[5]

I received a stack of old issues of *The Canadian Marksman*, and when I finally had an opportunity to look through them, I came across an article written by Gil Boa in 1957.[6] Gilmour Boa is the only man in the world to have won both the Queen's Prize and a World Smallbore Championship, not to mention three Queen's Medals in Service Rifle, the Governor General's Prize, as well as several Canadian championships in both smallbore and fullbore. Although the article was written nearly half a century ago, when people had to shoot with .303s as issued except for the back sights, there are parts you could quote in the next edition of your book on wind doping. Here are some of the points that I selected from Gil's article [plus some the authors of this book thought were worth repeating]:

- Whenever riflemen get together, there are long-winded discussions regarding the relative importance of various factors in marksmanship to success in competition. Among the items usually mentioned are good eyesight, steady nerves, physique, rifle accuracy—a subject in itself—ammunition, wind-judging ability, coaching, weather conditions, diet, training habits, the misfortune of being squadded with a slow shooter, and female competitors in tight pants. In my considered opinion, the most important factor, and the one most commonly overlooked by tyro and expert alike, is the ability to hold, aim correctly, and deliver the shot when the sight picture is perfect.

- It is, of course, impossible to make consistently good scores with a poor rifle. It is even more unlikely that a shooter will achieve satisfactory results, even with the finest rifle on the range, unless he is capable of holding it perfectly steady while he aims and fires the shot.

- Wind judging, at least under conditions normally encountered at Connaught Ranges, is a highly over-rated ability. The fact is that if we would leave our sights alone, our scores would frequently improve. If anyone doubts this statement, he has only to refer to his own scorebook and estimate what his scores would be with fewer windage changes.

- As for training habits, it is self-evident that a man who keeps in good condition, takes enough exercise to develop stamina, gets adequate rest, and eats and drinks in moderation will be more likely to endure successfully the rigors of a long program than a soft, self-indulgent person. This factor is demonstrated annually toward the end of the program, when certain individuals begin their celebrations a little too early on winning a place on the Bisley Team.

- Other factors, such as weather conditions, squadding, ammunition, and so forth, are beyond the control of the competitor. In a long aggregate they are practically equal for all.

- Thus we return to the all-important consideration, namely, to hold, aim, and fire the shots with such precision that almost all personal error is eliminated.

WORDS OF WISDOM
SMALLBORE WIND-READING
LINDA K MILLER

When the first edition of *The Wind Book* was published, it was met with great enthusiasm from the shooting community . . . except for one reader who was looking for information about reading the wind for Olympic-style smallbore. It was ironic because I had started in that discipline, but had not specifically included it in the book. *The Wind Book* is largely a reflection of my journey from

50-meter smallbore to 300- to 900-meter fullbore, written to help shooters new to long-range shooting to get through the learning curve.

With the second edition, I decided to cover a little bit about smallbore wind-reading.

I looked through the details of the first edition, looking for what I needed to add to address the idiosyncrasies of smallbore. Wind basics? They are the same. The thought process? The same. The techniques and tactics? Yes, the same. The underlying skills? The same.

But there are two things that are different about smallbore: one is the type of range and the other is the type of flags.

SMALLBORE RANGES

Olympic-Style 50-meter ranges are usually described as a "bowl" because they have some type of wall on at least three and sometimes all four sides. I like to visualize it like a fish tank, with the ripples bouncing between walls until they are resolved or until a larger force overpowers them.

No matter how you visualize it, it's important to see the wind as a continuous force that must enter, act, and usually exit the range. (Sometimes the wind doesn't so much exit the range as it dissipates somewhere in the range.) This gives you a good picture of the overall behavior of the air currents you're going to be dealing with. You may find it helpful to divide the range into thirds: the band closest to you, the mid-section, and the target end of the range. It's usually easiest to read the mid-section, but the band closest to you has the greatest effect on the bullet.

One of my wake-up calls was during a World Cup where the flags were just crazy. There didn't seem to be a rhyme or reason with their behavior, at least nothing I could latch on to. They looked like you could read them, but no! During sighters, I'd fire a shot expecting one thing and get something completely different.

Finally, I noticed a small round-leaf ground cover right in front of the firing line . . . it was describing the wind conditions accurately and eloquently. I used that little ground-cover for the rest of the match, and it was effective enough to put me on the medal podium.

Once you've got a good picture of the overall wind conditions on the range, you assess the particular behavior on your own line of fire. I've always found it easiest to be in the middle of the range, or somewhat downwind of center, because you can more easily see what wind is coming to you and more easily predict what will be happening by the time you fire your shot. If you are shooting on a firing point that's close to where the wind is sweeping into the range, it may not have as much lateral force, but you may have to deal with some vertical displacement. I think the most challenging place on the range is where the wind is exiting . . . you do have the full width of the range to see the wind coming, but you must deal with (sometimes unpredictable) swirling as the wind hits the wall and curls back over that side of the range.

In headwind/tailwind range situations, the most critical thing is usually small variations in wind direction, just as it is in fullbore. If you have right wind correction on and the wind shifts to the other side of center, you suddenly have a double error.

In fact, I can certainly understand why so many fullbore shooters use smallbore for cross-training. Nowadays the range conditions are getting more similar, as fullbore ranges are often surrounded by big berms that cause a similar "bowl" effect on the wind currents.

Everything you learned in smallbore can be transferred to fullbore; indeed, those things can also be transferred to Extreme Long-Range shooting. Reading the terrain, dividing the range into behavior-zones, assessing the characteristics of your particular line of fire . . . all good skills to hone, no matter your shooting discipline.

SMALLBORE FLAGS

One of the key things that was lacking in my training in smallbore was any attempt to put a specific value on the flags. The instruction I got was to get a general feel for the conditions during sighters (which are unlimited) and test your intuitions during that time.

Once I had transitioned to the fullbore world, I realized that I had not known very much about reading smallbore flags. An opportunity arose when I was coaching the Canadian Women's CISM Rifle Team. CISM (International Military Sports Council or Conseil International du Sport Militaire) is a multi-disciplinary sports organization, and one of the disciplines is Olympic-style smallbore. As it happened, all the members of my team were both smallbore and fullbore competitors, so we decided to approach flag-reading just as we would in fullbore.

The flags are little strips of silk or synthetic, and while their characteristics are tightly defined by the International Olympic Committee, at non-Olympic events, they can vary, but we had to start somewhere. First, we had to know what value our little silk strips had.

Since there are many smallbore rifle sights with different "click" values (and most of the sights can't be easily used to read a setting from the dial), I decided the easiest thing would be to correlate the behavior of the flags directly to the behavior of the bullet. So, we conducted trials.

Each shooter was given a wind coach. The wind coach watched the flags and ordered the shooter to fire when the flags were in the condition we were testing. First, they made sure the shooter was properly zeroed for a no-wind condition. We tested three conditions with a pure crosswind: the flags lifted to 90 degrees, the flags lifted to about 60 degrees, and the flags lifted to about 30 degrees. You can appreciate that all of this was approximate, but the results were still revealing:

- The 90-degree flag displaced the bullet to the 7-ring;
- The 60-degree flag displaced the bullet to the 8-ring;
- The 30-dgree flag displaced the bullet to the 9-ring.

Now you only need to know how many clicks your particular sight needs to correct for each. (You can start with the information that came with your sight, which usually gives

FIG: 72b: 90-degree flag.

FIG: 72a: Shooter with wind coach.

FIG: 72c: 60-degree flag.

FIG: 72d: 30-degree flag.

the number of clicks to move a specific distance; for example, 10 clicks per centimeter.)

Once you have this little bit of information, you can use it as a base to springboard your skill at wind-reading. The techniques, skills, and tactics described elsewhere in this book can be applied to improve your learning . . . and your scores.

NEW SMALLBORE EVENTS

One of the smallbore events that's currently popular is "Rimfire PRS" . . . a smallbore version of the very popular fullbore "Precision Rifle Series." The general idea is requiring the shooter to use unconventional (somewhat rested) positions at irregular distances out to about 300 meters.

Wind-reading at these events is difficult because there are no flags. However, just as in any shooting event, there are other indicators such as feel, dust, grass, and trees; and mirage is an effective tool, as are the fall-of-shot of other competitors.

CONCLUSION

Every time you shoot, each shot can contribute to your understanding of reading the wind. Whether the shot lands where you expect (confirming your assessment and solution were correct), or whether the shot lands elsewhere . . . every shot and its outcome is data, data you can use to inform your understanding and your next decision.

ARNOLD PARKS, CANADA
WINNER OF THE QUEEN'S PRIZE AT BISLEY (1968)
MEMBER OF DCRA HALL OF FAME

When I was shooting in Ottawa during the 1950s, I usually had short-range scores that would place me on the Bisley Team; however, my long-range scores left something to be desired and as a result I would miss the team. After much trial and error, and discussions with several good shooters, I came up with two principles to follow when shooting long ranges and they appeared to work for me.

1. A shooter should take his wind readings from one or two flags that are close to the firing point and not get confused by trying to read all the flags downrange. (Naturally, correctly reading the flags comes with experience.)
2. Once the shooter decides on the required sight setting, the shooter should shoot fast and not hold for a lengthy period. I found that when shooting fast one might drop a point for elevation, but one point lost high or low is better than holding for a long period and dropping two or three points (or missing altogether) due to a wind change.

I might mention that when I won the Governor's for the second time in 1975, it was mostly a mirage shoot at 1,000 yards with continual changes, from the right one second and from the left the next minute and sometimes boiling. The chap who marked my scorecard mentioned after the shoot that he timed my last nine shots: from the time I moved my eye away from the spotting scope to the time I fired, I averaged nine seconds. During the nine seconds I adjusted my sight for the required windage.

JIM PATON, CANADA
WINNER OF THE QUEEN'S PRIZE AT BISLEY (2005)
MEMBER OF DCRA HALL OF FAME

[Authors' note: The following brief notes are the result of a short conversation that Jim had with us last summer. He is one of the great wind readers who finds it difficult to articulate exactly what they do. We appreciate his words of wisdom; though brief, they are meaningful.]

If I were to give a bit of advice on wind reading to new shooters, I would say three things:

1. Learn about, understand, and act on the facts (the science and the math) of wind reading. For example, every shooter should know the value difference between a 1 o'clock and a 2 o'clock wind.
2. Get a mentor. There is no substitute for having someone knowledgeable and experienced close at hand to help you understand the small points, and the big points, too.
3. Do autopsies. Review every lesson you have learned, and review again to get the last bit of information out of your experiences. Be dispassionate; just look for lessons that you can apply in future shoots.

SANDY PEDEN, CANADA
MEMBER OF DCRA HALL OF FAME

One of the things that I have always found helpful is to study the conditions and terrain before it is my turn to shoot. If one is about to shoot on a strange range, studying the terrain surrounding the range has always been a help. It gives you an idea of where the danger spots may be. Study the previous shooters in action as well. If you think you see a change, watch the butts for the results of that change.

It is essential to have a high-quality scope that will show you eight to ten targets at 1,000 yards. That way you get a quicker look at the results of changes. When you are shooting in difficult conditions, always keep a watch on the upwind targets. A good scope allows you to do this easily.

On Connaught, there are plenty of flags to give you strength and angle. One of the methods I use in spotting changes is to pick out two flags and watch the tips. You will find that when you are in the prone position, the tips of the flags will always be pointing at one of the distant target number boards. As long as the tip keeps pointing at the same number, you don't have to do much. If it changes, it is easy to see. And using a Plot-o-Matic (EZ-Graf) is a good way to confirm the fact

that you may not have to do much or to identify that you may have to deal with several conditions.

ED POCOCK III, UNITED STATES

[Authors' note: Ed Pocock is the author of "All You Need to Know About Wind," quoted elsewhere in this book. We asked him for additional words of wisdom, and this is what he said.]

I think that the best thing that a new long-range shooter can do is find a person who actually knows *how* to read the wind and then convert that to *proper* sight adjustments. Coaching is the key to success, and bad coaching is a path to despair and aggravation.

Also, shooters must *trust* their calls. So many people try to "Kentucky windage" their guns, as opposed to making a call, firing, and then analyzing that shot. *Learn* from the bad calls and relish the good ones—a shooter wins in both cases.

BILL RICHARDS, GREAT BRITAIN
COACH ON WINNING GB PALMA TEAMS
OF 1992 AND 1995

I'm not sure that I use a specific thought process per se, in that I am of the school that believes much of reading the wind is at a nontechnical, subconscious/experiential level. Or to put it another way, I make use of my stored experiences to guide me. What I can say is that I try to take in the range as a whole and try to avoid relying on specific indicators. I will quite often work mainly off a type of indicator—flags or mirage depending on the conditions, but I will always take into account what other indicators are telling me. Here are a few tips that I tell people on my courses.

Have Confidence in Yourself

Avoid using "wind aids"; have confidence in yourself. In many countries, the UK included, you can buy what are called "wind calculators" or purchase plot sheets with pretty little flag diagrams. In the USA you are even allowed personal anemometers, which can be used to tell you what the wind speed is. In all cases, such devices are only able to give you an approximate guide as to what to put on your sight. After no more than a season or two on the range, most people are able to make an educated guess that is as accurate or better than these tools (whether they believe it or not). Worse still, regular use of these tools leads to a kind of dependency, a crutch without which the shooter feels lost. However, by their very use, the shooter's own progress in developing real wind-reading skills is significantly hindered, since they are more likely to reach for their calculator than their own knowledge.

Use Your Own Eyes

Don't believe everything you hear; use your own eyes. You are walking out onto the range and you meet a friend coming off: "I'd not bother with the flags; the mirage was much more accurate," or "I found the mirage completely useless" is his cheerful comment. This presupposes that you both perceive mirage and flags in the same way and that the conditions will be the same when you lie down. The flags might have been "misreading" for him because he wasn't looking at the "right" flags, or the flags were a little damp and were therefore not reading their true strength, or he may well focus his scope at a different part of the range for mirage.

Reading the Wind Is Not an Exact Science

Many people spend too long trying to decide exactly what the wind is. Putting 3 or 3½ MOA) on your sight at most distances will probably result in no difference to your score. The difference in *making up your mind* between these two values may well be worth a point or more. I don't know of anyone who can regularly read the wind beyond 600 yards to the nearest quarter—occasionally, maybe; regularly, no. Make your decision and live with it; that isn't to say that your decision shouldn't be to wait, albeit in some countries that will be for only 20 to 30 seconds. Indecision leads to your not being confident about your sight setting, which in turn affects your performance; more importantly, it usually means that the time between your putting the wind on your sight and taking the shot is increased, which means that the wind has more time to change.

Keep Your Eyes on the Wind

This may sound really obvious, but many people spend time doing elevation and wind graphs and a host of other "book work." If you have your head in a scorebook, who is watching the wind? Try to keep such things to a minimum; many people dispense with a scorebook altogether in string shooting. Keep your eyes on the flags/mirage, etc., and not in a book. Most teams in international matches use plotters for maintaining the scorebook and drawing graphs, to allow the coach to concentrate on the conditions; learn from this.

Trust Your Instincts

There are those days when the flags appear to be moving exactly as they were for the previous shot, the mirage is still running the same as it was before, but some nagging doubt tells you that the wind has changed. Believe it. More than likely, it is your stored experience feeding your subconscious, trying desperately to tell you that the wind has indeed changed. The more experience you have, the more you can (and should) rely on "gut feeling."

Using Flags and/or Mirage

I have to admit that I am a bigger fan of flags than mirage, for a whole host of reasons. Here are the main ones:

1. Mirage depends on sunlight and water. In this country [UK], we have too little of the former and too much of the latter; the end result is we don't often get mirage because it is too cold or overcast, and when we do get mirage, it typically disappears at midafternoon.

2. I have never found mirage to be particularly accurate when the wind gets much above light. I have used mirage up to around 4 minutes at 600, but much above that it starts getting difficult to judge the magnitude of the wind. Sure, you can tell there has been a change, but I find it really tough trying to quantify it. It could well be that I simply don't often have the opportunity to improve my mirage reading.

3. Mirage is line of sight. At long range this means that what you are usually viewing through your scope is some

way below the path of the bullet. (I know that flags are typically above the path, but air at ground level suffers from what I call being "sticky"—it seems to have more inertia and I typically find that flags show the change ahead of the mirage.)

4. Mirage is *"now"* wind. Again, because what you are looking at is wind directly between you and your target, mirage is an instantaneous view of what the wind is doing, often in a relatively small section of the range, defined by where you are focusing and the depth of field of your scope. Unless you have a perfectly flat, featureless range, including the area around the range for several hundred yards, mirage is not a very fair reflection of future wind.

Flags have their drawbacks too, but they do tell you futures, which is why I think they are of far better value. I can't look through my scope, change my sight, and fire a good shot in much under five seconds in individual shooting. With flags, I can judge how fast the change I have observed is moving toward me, I can then either shoot or I can put it on the sight, wait a few seconds, and then shoot; either way I find it more accurate.

This isn't to say that I don't use mirage; I do, but it is pretty rare that I only use mirage (or just flags for that matter).

As far as where to focus your scope, old man Newton dictates that the wind nearest you is the most important, so most people are taught to focus their scopes 100–200 yards in front of the firing point. Much closer than this, and you can barely make out the target for the purposes of spotting your shot, especially on a "heavy" day.

The only time I go for a longer focus is when the wind is coming from the direction of the targets, since focusing nearer the targets will give you some measure of futures (the only time mirage can).

The quality of your scope makes a much bigger difference than people sometimes think. It is only when you look

through a Kowa TSN-1, with its 77mm objective lens or similar scope that you appreciate just how much you don't see through your lightweight 50mm scope. Also, make sure you don't go any higher than a 25X power; any more and you see less, not more, mirage.

A good stand is also essential, especially if you coach from a chair; when the scope is waving around, it is much harder to accurately judge changes in the mirage.

As far as knowing what wind to put on for what mirage, never forget that if you see a change on the mirage there are likely to be people shooting at the same time who haven't. As such, if you are unable to judge how much the wind has changed, take a view off some of the surrounding targets.

I often will make a note on my scorecard about what I think the wind is when I actually fire the shot, as well as what I have on the sights. This reinforces the accuracy of your wind reading and, in my experience, is especially true for reading mirage.

In the end, the only way of learning how to read the wind is to get out there and make mistakes and then learn from them.

JOHN C. SIMPSON, UNITED STATES

[Authors' note: John Simpson is the author of "The Question is Blowin' in the Wind," quoted elsewhere in this book. We asked him for additional words of wisdom, and this is what he said.]

The First Thing

Students need to realize that when we talk about adjusting the sights to "move the strike of the round" we are engaging in a convenient fiction. What we are in fact moving with our sights is the center of the potential shot group. What the wind is moving is the center of that same potential shot group. Mastery of this will help prevent the tendency to chase the spotters all over the target during slow fire.

As an example, I recently saw a written test from a police sniper school that had this question: "You are shooting at a 300-yard target. The bullet impacts the target 3 inches to the left of center. How hard is the wind blowing?"

The author of that question just doesn't "get it." Given most people's dispersion (or shot group size), a single shot can reasonably wind up 3 inches from the point of aim on a no-wind day.

It's easy to become flippant in trying to impart the intangibles of "doping" the wind. While working as an instructor at the Special Operations Target Interdiction Course at Fort Bragg, I was assigned with another instructor named Sfc. George Miller. What George and I wanted to do was inspired by the Val Kilmer movie *Willow*. We started collecting and cleaning different small-animal bones. When a sniper student would give up, turn around, and ask us what the wind was doing we would "throw the bones," study them for a bit, and then solemnly announce, "Three clicks left."

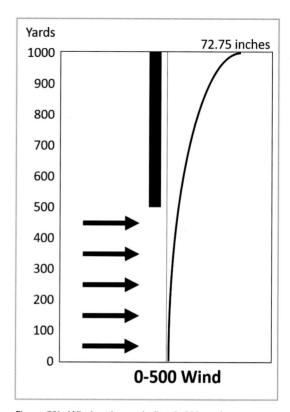

Figure 73b: Wind acting on bullet, 0–500 yards.

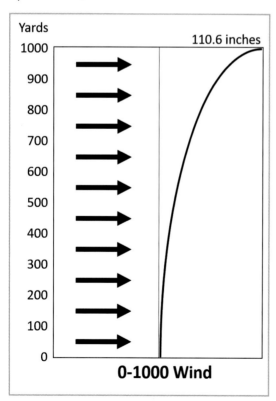

Figure 73a: Wind acting on bullet, 0–1,000 yards.

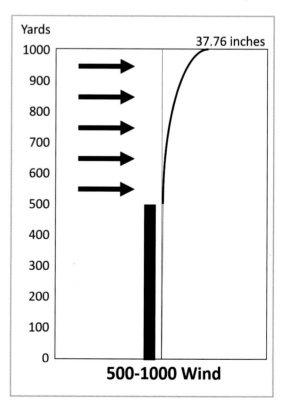

Figure 74. Wind acting on bullet, 500–1,000 yards.

[Authors' note: on a more serious tone, in "The Question Is Blowin' in the Wind," John Simpson included the above diagrams based on .308 Winchester. They show some real numbers to demonstrate that the near wind results in more deflection than the far wind. He says they are his own version of the ones in Canadian Bisley Shooting.]

PAT VAMPLEW, CANADA
MEMBER OF DCRA HALL OF FAME

Learning from the Masters

Imagine looking downrange at the range flags, assessing the wind, changing your sights, firing the perfect shot, and looking through your scope to see a perfect bull's-eye! What a thrill for the target rifle shooter. To the casual observer, an experienced marksman makes the whole process look so easy and simple. To the beginning marksman, the wind can be your worst enemy.

The inexperienced marksman should learn the wind techniques from a variety of high-performance shooters. By learning various strategies, the shooter can gather an assortment of tools and techniques for attacking and challenging the wind.

When I was a young shooter, with wind chart in tow, my idols Gerry Ouellette, Gil Boa, Arnold Parks, and Des Burke spent many hours trying to explain and outline the basics of the range winds. The general rules were kept simple, but Des Burke made sure that I knew the difference between sine and cosine formulas!

Here are some of these tips that may help you in your shooting against the wind.

- Wind is basically judged by strength and direction. Direction is often associated with the clock, given in the form of where the wind comes from (e.g., a wind from the NNW is an 11 o'clock wind). Strength is often judged in miles per hour. Using wind flags, a different wind strength is assigned every 4 mph. For example, a 20-mph flag is blowing horizontal to the ground. Usually, the tip of the flag will indicate the actual strength of the wind. The more horizontal the tip, the stronger the wind.

- Along with strength and direction, a shooter must peer through his telescope to see a phenomenon called mirage. More experienced shooters use the mirage to judge wind rather than strength and direction. The mirage is a mass of air that is heated by the ground as it passes by any given point. The mirage movement through one's scope is often in the form of a wave. The higher the amplitude of the wave, the less wind downrange. As the air speeds up, the amplitude decreases until a flat-like wave passes by the observer. This change in amplitude allows the shooter to be aware of a wind change. There are two limitations to the mirage. If a predominately cloudy day occurs, the mirage may not be visible. If the wind has a velocity that exceeds 12–16 mph, the mirage is flat and it is very hard to distinguish a noticeable change in velocity.

- Knowledge of the wind chart is a must for the beginner. If the beginner can first recognize a change in the wind and then move the sights the proper amount, many points will be saved/acquired! All beginning shooters should carry their wind charts in their shooting boxes, so that an approximate amount of minutes can be put on the sight before the shoot begins. Once the shoot begins, if the shooter keeps the following numbers in their mental toolbox, then half the battle of judging the wind is done.

Wind Factor Chart

The wind factor chart below is very compact and easy-to-memorize. The numbers in it are strength changes at a given angle of the wind. These values are given for a gentle (4-mph) wind.[7]

- For example, if the shooter is at 500 yards, and there is a 4-mph wind coming from 1 o'clock, the shooter uses

¾ minute of wind . . . and every time the wind strength increases or decreases, the shooter should move the sight ¾ of a minute. If the wind goes up another 4 mph, then the shooter needs to add another ¾ of a minute on the sight.

- Again at 500 yards, if the wind is coming from 2 o'clock, the shooter uses 1½ minutes of wind and adds 1½ minutes for every additional 4 mph of wind, as shown in Figure 76.

Other wind indicators that shooters may use: watch the direction of muzzle gas, throw grass into the air to confirm wind direction, keep track of the angle of rain . . . whether it be a mist or downpour! Finally, keep an eye through your scope just before it is your turn to shoot. If you think there is a change in the wind, wait 15 seconds and look through the scope to see whether there are tendencies of other good shooters who may be up- or downwind from a normal bull's-eye pattern.

	1 o'clock	2 o'clock	3 o'clock
300 m	½ min	1 min	1½ min
500 y	¾ min	1½ min	2 min
600 y	1 min	2 min	2½ min
800 m	1½ min	2½ min	3½ min
900 m	2 min	3 min	4 min

Figure 75. Wind factor chart.

		1 o'clock	2 o'clock	3 o'clock
Gentle	4 mph	¾ min	1½ min	2 min
Moderate	8 mph	1½ min	3 min	4 min
Fresh	12 mph	2¼ min	4½ min	6 min
Strong	16 mph	3 min	6 min	8 min
Very Strong	20 mph	3¾ min	7½ min	10 min

Figure 76. Wind example chart for 500 yards.

In order to get experience in judging the wind, a shooter must keep practicing judging the wind. During practice, make mistakes. Try moving the sights. Leave your sights alone and watch where the bullets go from the previous shot.

Watch other good shooters after you have finished shooting.

In conclusion, if you establish a shooting routine on the shooting mound for the wind itself, you will become more aware of what you and your fellow competitors are doing to combat the wind. When your turn comes around to shoot, check the flags for direction and strength, check the mirage through your scope, and fire the perfect shot every time. Check the flags and mirage again to confirm your original plan. As Des Burke told me when I was young, "The wind can be your best friend, or it can be your worst enemy." The wind is my friend!

MIKE WONG SHUI, CANADA MEMBER OF DCRA HALL OF FAME

Authors: *When you first arrive at the range for a match, what do you look at and what do you think about?*
MWS: Usually, when I first arrive at the range, I am trying to see if the targets are visible and if I require filters, rain gear, etc. Also I check, if any flags are available, what are the estimates with the charts I have. If I am not shooting first, then hopefully someone will let me know if my starting guess will be in the right ballpark.

I am also trying to determine if my preparation (equipment, etc.) is all done, or if I overlooked anything.

Authors: *When you are preparing to set your sight for that first sighter, what do you think about in order to make that decision?*
MWS: I will then be going through my checklist to make sure the elevation is correct and my position is stable; find out what I can actually see from where I am shooting, how much change has occurred since I made my prediction using the charts. [I also] check if there is anyone around me who will give reliable indication of the trends.

A good shot is essential here, so all the time required to produce a clean shot must be taken.

Authors: *When you have the results from your first sighter, what do you think about in order to set your sight for the second sighter?*

MWS: I will usually correct to center and then see if there was any change in conditions. After the first few shots, I will be trying to locate the center of the group and the extremes. Unless really called for, I will not move much past the extremes already encountered. Conditions really dictate whether I will be trying to shoot for the center each time, or will I be just trying to stay in the black.

CHARLES F. YOUNG, GREAT BRITAIN

[Authors' note: Charles Young is the author of "Wind Reading—Another Way of Looking at It?" quoted elsewhere in this book. We asked him for additional words of wisdom, and this is what he said.]

Wind reading is so intuitive . . . that old farts (like me) can cope quite well, and it may make up for our eyesight problems and stiff joints, but only if the wind's blowing!

CONCLUSION

Having now spent several years focusing on the subject of wind reading as something teachable, we have come to one important conclusion: *learning to read the wind is like learning to play chess.*

When you learn to play chess, you learn the rules of the game and the capabilities of the pieces. You will probably pick up a book and learn about the standard gambits of the masters. You may even deepen your reading and find out that the masters do not plot out the moves analytically, but rather they look for patterns of strength on the board. In fact, you may even play a little "duplicate chess," replaying the masters' moves and learning from analyzing their games. But, one day, in order to learn to play chess, you must sit down at the board and make your moves. You will learn as much from missteps as you do from successes. Over days, and weeks, and years, you will deepen your experience until one day, you will make ultimately successful moves without completely knowing why. You will have become the master.

In this book you will find all the information you need to learn to read the wind. We have presented the facts, as we understand them, in clear laymen's terms, with lots of diagrams and pictures. We have talked about the techniques and tactics that can be applied to various wind situations. We have analyzed the skills it takes to become a top-notch wind reader. We have gone to the masters and brought you their words of wisdom.

And, as in chess, we believe there are three secrets to achieving mastery:

* Pattern recognition
* Memory
* Focus on the one right thing

But, one day, in order to learn to read the wind, you must get down behind your gun and make your moves.

APPENDIX A: TOOLS

"Knowledge is the most democratic source of power."
—Alvin Toffler

The following pages are designed so that you can copy them and use them as your own tools. Here's what we've included:

- Wind description table
- Our wind value and wind deflection charts
- Our wind diagrams
- A metric-English conversion table

Standard Terms	Mph	Kph	Ft/ sec	Observations	Flag Description	Flag Angle	Flag	Mirage Description	Mirage
Calm	0-1	0-2	0-2	Calm. Smoke rises vertically.	Flag hangs limply on the pole			Boiling. Streamers flowing upwards with no lateral movement	*Boiling*
Light Air	1-3	2-5	2-4	Light air. Smoke drifts slowly. Barely felt.	Flag moves to the lee side of pole			Leaning. Mostly upward movement, but starting to "lean" enough to clearly depict direction of wind	*Leaning*
Gentle	4	6	6	Slight breeze. Leaves rustle. Felt on face.	Flag lifts off the pole and flutters	15 degrees		Flowing gently. Clearly horizontal flow in big waves, moving loosely and slowly.	*Flowing Gently*
Moderate	8	13	12	Moderate breeze. Leaves & twigs in motion.	Flag is definitely clear of the pole	30 degrees		Flowing rapidly. Streamers flowing horizontally with small waves, close together.	*Flowing Rapidly*
Fresh	12	19	18	Fresh breeze. Small branches move.	Flag center-line is usually clearly visible	60 degrees		Slick. Mirage streaming quickly. Difficult to see changes. Flatlining	*Streaming to Flatlining*
Strong	16	25	24	Strong breeze. Small trees sway.	Flag is straight out and getting "starched"	90 degrees		Mirage gone	
Very Strong	20	32	29	Very strong breeze. Large branches sway.	The fewer the ripples, the faster the wind	Above horizontal			

Figure 77. Wind description table.

SPEED	Kph	5	10	15	20	25	30	35	40	45	50
DIRECTION	Mph	3	6	9	12	15	18	22	25	28	31
Degrees	O'clock										
0	12:00, 6:00	0	0	0	0	0	0	0	0	0	0
10		1	1	2	2	3	3	4	4	5	5
15	11:30, 12:30, 5:30, 6:30	1	2	2	3	4	5	6	6	7	8
20		1	2	3	4	5	6	8	9	10	11
30	11:00, 1:00, 5:00, 7:00	2	3	5	6	8	9	11	13	14	16
40		2	4	6	8	10	12	14	16	18	20
45	10:30, 1:30 4:30, 7:30	2	4	7	9	11	13	16	18	20	22
50		2	5	7	10	12	14	17	19	21	24
60	10:00, 2:00, 4:00, 8:00	3	5	8	11	13	16	19	22	24	27
70		3	6	9	12	15	17	21	24	26	29
75	2:30, 3:30, 8:30, 9:30	3	6	9	12	15	18	21	24	27	30
80		3	6	9	12	15	18	22	25	28	31
90	3:00, 9:00	3	6	9	12	15	18	22	25	28	31

Figure 78. Wind value conversion.

In Kph and Mph

Wind Value	Range in Yards									
	100	200	300	400	500	600	700	800	900	1000
1	.1	.1	.2	.3	.3	.4	.5	.6	.7	.9
2	.1	.3	.4	.5	.7	.9	1.0	1.2	1.5	1.7
3	.2	.4	.6	.8	1.0	1.3	1.6	1.9	2.2	2.5
4	.2	.5	.8	1.0	1.4	1.7	2.1	2.5	2.9	3.4
5	.3	.6	1.0	1.3	1.7	2.1	2.6	3.1	3.6	4.2
6	.4	.7	1.1	1.6	2.0	2.6	3.1	3.7	4.4	5.1
7	.4	.9	1.3	1.8	2.4	3.0	3.6	4.3	5.1	5.9
8	.5	1.0	1.5	2.1	2.7	3.4	4.1	4.9	5.8	6.8
9	.5	1.1	1.7	2.4	3.1	3.8	4.6	5.5	6.5	7.6
10	.6	1.2	1.9	2.6	3.4	4.3	5.2	6.2	7.3	8.5
11	.7	1.3	2.1	2.9	3.7	4.7	5.7	6.8	8.0	9.3
12	.7	1.5	2.3	3.1	4.1	5.5	6.2	7.4	8.7	10.2
13	.8	1.6	2.5	3.4	4.4	5.5	6.7	8.0	9.4	11.0
14	.8	1.7	2.7	3.7	4.8	5.9	7.2	8.6	10.2	11.8
15	.9	1.8	2.8	3.9	5.1	6.4	7.7	9.2	10.9	12.7
16	.9	2.0	3.0	4.2	5.4	6.8	8.3	9.9	11.6	13.5
17	1.0	2.1	3.2	4.5	5.8	7.2	8.8	10.5	12.3	14.4
18	1.1	2.2	3.4	4.7	6.1	7.6	9.3	11.1	13.1	15.2
19	1.1	2.3	3.6	5.0	6.5	8.1	9.8	11.7	13.8	16.1
20	1.2	2.4	3.8	5.2	6.8	8.5	10.3	12.3	14.5	16.9
21	1.2	2.6	4.0	5.5	7.1	8.9	10.8	12.9	15.3	17.8
22	1.3	2.7	4.2	5.8	7.5	9.3	11.4	13.6	16.0	18.6
23	1.4	2.8	4.4	6.0	7.8	9.8	11.9	14.2	16.7	19.5
24	1.4	2.9	4.5	6.3	8.2	10.2	12.4	14.8	17.4	20.3
25	1.5	3.1	4.7	6.5	8.5	10.6	12.9	15.4	18.2	21.2
26	1.5	3.2	4.9	6.8	8.8	11.0	13.4	16.0	18.9	22.0
27	1.6	3.3	5.1	7.1	9.2	11.5	13.9	16.6	19.6	22.8
28	1.7	3.4	5.3	7.3	9.5	11.9	14.5	17.3	20.3	23.7
29	1.7	3.5	5.5	7.6	9.9	12.3	15.0	17.9	21.1	24.5
30	1.8	3.7	5.7	7.9	10.2	12.8	15.5	18.5	21.8	25.4
31	1.8	3.8	5.9	8.1	10.6	13.2	16.0	19.1	22.5	26.2

Figure 79. Windage chart for 155-grain .308 Match—Yards—MOA.

155-g Sierra MK; MV 3100 fps; BC .455; Temp 77°F; Elevation 600 ft

Wind Value	Range in Meters								
	100	200	300	400	500	600	700	800	900
1	.1	.1	.2	.3	.4	.5	.6	.7	.8
2	.1	.3	.4	.6	.8	1.0	1.2	1.4	1.6
3	.2	.4	.6	.9	1.1	1.4	1.7	2.1	2.5
4	.3	.5	.8	1.2	1.5	1.9	2.3	2.8	3.3
5	.3	.7	1.0	1.5	1.9	2.4	2.9	3.5	4.1
6	.4	.8	1.3	1.7	2.3	2.8	3.5	4.2	4.9
7	.5	.9	1.5	2.0	2.6	3.3	4.0	4.9	5.8
8	.5	1.1	1.7	2.3	3.0	3.8	4.6	5.6	6.6
9	.6	1.2	1.9	2.6	3.4	4.3	5.2	6.2	7.4
10	.7	1.3	2.1	2.9	3.8	4.7	5.8	6.9	8.2
11	.7	1.5	2.3	3.2	4.2	5.2	6.4	7.6	9.0
12	.8	1.6	2.5	3.5	4.5	5.7	6.9	8.3	9.9
13	.8	1.7	2.7	3.8	4.9	6.2	7.5	9.0	10.7
14	.9	1.9	2.9	4.0	5.3	6.6	8.1	9.7	11.5
15	1.0	2.0	3.1	4.3	5.7	7.1	8.7	10.4	12.3
16	1.0	2.1	3.3	4.6	6.0	7.6	9.2	11.1	13.2
17	1.1	2.3	3.5	4.9	6.4	8.0	9.8	11.8	14.0
18	1.2	2.4	3.7	5.2	6.8	8.5	10.4	12.5	14.8
19	1.2	2.5	4.0	5.5	7.2	9.0	11.0	13.2	15.6
20	1.3	2.7	4.2	5.8	7.5	9.5	11.6	13.9	16.4
21	1.4	2.8	4.4	6.1	7.9	9.9	12.1	14.6	17.3
22	1.4	2.9	4.6	6.4	8.3	10.4	12.7	15.3	18.1
23	1.5	3.1	4.8	6.6	8.7	10.9	13.3	16.0	18.9
24	1.5	3.2	5.0	6.9	9.0	11.3	13.9	16.7	19.7
25	1.6	3.3	5.2	7.2	9.4	11.8	14.4	17.3	20.5
26	1.7	3.5	5.4	7.5	9.8	12.3	15.0	18.0	21.4
27	1.7	3.6	5.6	7.8	10.2	12.8	15.6	18.7	22.2
28	1.8	3.7	5.8	8.1	10.6	13.2	16.2	19.4	23.0
29	1.9	3.9	6.0	8.4	10.9	13.7	16.8	20.2	23.8
30	1.9	4.0	6.2	8.7	11.3	14.2	17.3	20.8	24.7
31	2.0	4.1	6.4	9.0	11.7	14.7	17.9	21.5	25.5

Figure 80. Windage Chart for 155-grain .308 Match—Meters—MOA.

155-g Sierra MK; MV 3100 fps; BC .455; Temp 77°F; Elevation 600 ft

Wind Value	Range in Yards									
	100	200	300	400	500	600	700	800	900	1000
1	0.1	0.1	0.2	0.3	0.4	0.6	0.7	0.8	1.0	1.1
2	0.2	0.3	0.5	0.7	0.9	1.1	1.4	1.7	2.0	2.3
3	0.2	0.5	0.7	1.1	1.4	1.7	2.1	2.6	3.0	3.5
4	0.3	0.6	1.0	1.4	1.9	2.3	2.9	3.4	4.0	4.7
5	0.4	0.8	1.3	1.8	2.3	2.9	3.6	4.3	5.1	5.8
6	0.5	1.0	1.5	2.1	2.8	3.5	4.3	5.2	6.1	7.0
7	0.6	1.1	1.8	2.5	3.3	4.1	5.0	6.0	7.1	8.2
8	0.6	1.3	2.1	2.9	3.7	4.7	5.8	6.9	8.1	9.4
9	0.7	1.5	2.3	3.2	4.2	5.3	6.5	7.8	9.1	10.6
10	0.8	1.6	2.6	3.6	4.7	5.9	7.2	8.6	10.2	11.9
11	0.9	1.8	2.8	4.0	5.2	6.5	7.9	9.5	11.2	12.9
12	1.0	2.0	3.1	4.3	5.6	7.1	8.7	10.4	12.2	14.1
13	1.0	2.1	3.4	4.7	6.1	7.7	9.4	11.2	13.2	15.3
14	1.1	2.3	3.6	5.0	6.6	8.3	10.1	12.1	14.2	16.5
15	1.2	2.5	3.9	5.4	7.1	8.9	10.8	13.0	15.3	17.8
16	1.3	2.6	4.1	5.8	7.5	9.4	11.6	13.8	16.3	18.8
17	1.4	2.8	4.4	6.1	8.0	10.0	12.3	14.7	17.3	20.0
18	1.4	3.0	4.7	6.5	8.5	10.6	13.0	15.6	18.3	21.2
19	1.5	3.2	4.9	6.9	9.0	11.2	13.7	16.5	19.4	22.4
20	1.6	3.3	5.2	7.2	9.4	11.8	14.5	17.3	20.4	23.8
21	1.7	3.5	5.4	7.6	9.9	12.4	15.2	18.2	21.4	24.7
22	1.8	3.7	5.7	7.9	10.4	13.0	15.9	19.1	22.4	25.9
23	1.8	3.8	6.0	8.3	10.8	13.6	16.6	19.9	23.4	27.1
24	1.9	4.0	6.2	8.7	11.3	14.2	17.4	20.8	24.5	28.2
25	2.0	4.2	6.5	9.0	11.8	14.8	18.1	21.7	25.5	29.4
26	2.1	4.3	6.8	9.4	12.3	15.4	18.8	22.5	26.5	30.6
27	2.2	4.5	7.0	9.8	12.7	16.0	19.5	23.4	27.5	31.8
28	2.3	4.7	7.3	10.1	13.2	16.6	20.3	24.3	28.5	33.0
29	2.3	4.8	7.5	10.53	13.72	17.20	21.01	25.18	29.61	34.1
30	2.4	5.0	7.8	10.8	14.2	17.8	21.7	26.0	30.6	35.3
31	2.5	5.2	8.1	11.2	14.6	18.3	22.4	26.9	31.6	36.5

Figure 81. Windage Chart for 168-grain .308 Match—Yards—MOA.

168-grain Sierra MK; MV 2600 fps; BC .462; Temp 70°F; Elevation 600 ft

Wind Value	Range in Meters								
	100	200	300	400	500	600	700	800	900
1	0.0	0.1	0.2	0.4	0.5	0.6	0.8	0.9	1.1
2	0.1	0.3	0.5	0.7	1.0	1.3	1.6	1.9	2.2
3	0.2	0.5	0.8	1.2	1.5	1.9	2.4	2.9	3.4
4	0.3	0.7	1.1	1.6	2.1	2.6	3.2	3.9	4.5
5	0.4	0.9	1.4	2.0	2.6	3.3	4.0	4.8	5.7
6	0.5	1.0	1.7	2.4	3.1	3.9	4.8	5.8	6.8
7	0.6	1.2	2.0	2.7	3.6	4.6	5.6	6.8	8.0
8	0.7	1.4	2.3	3.2	4.2	5.2	6.5	7.8	9.1
9	0.8	1.6	2.5	3.6	4.7	5.9	7.3	8.7	10.3
10	0.9	1.8	2.8	4.0	5.2	6.6	8.1	9.7	11.4
11	1.0	2.0	3.1	4.4	5.7	7.2	8.9	10.7	12.6
12	1.0	2.1	3.4	4.8	6.3	7.9	9.7	11.7	13.7
13	1.1	2.3	3.7	5.2	6.8	8.6	10.5	12.6	14.9
14	1.2	2.5	4.0	5.6	7.3	9.2	11.3	13.6	15.7
15	1.2	2.7	4.3	6.0	7.8	9.9	12.1	14.6	17.2
16	1.3	2.9	4.6	6.4	8.4	10.5	13.0	15.6	18.3
17	1.4	3.0	4.8	6.8	8.9	11.2	13.8	16.6	19.5
18	1.5	3.2	5.1	7.2	9.4	11.9	14.6	17.5	20.6
19	1.6	3.5	5.4	7.6	9.9	12.5	15.4	18.5	21.8
20	1.7	3.6	5.7	8.0	10.5	13.2	16.2	19.5	22.9
21	1.8	3.8	6.0	8.4	11.0	13.8	17.0	20.5	24.1
22	1.9	4.0	6.3	8.8	11.5	14.5	17.8	21.4	25.2
23	2.0	4.2	6.6	9.2	12.0	15.2	18.7	22.4	26.3
24	2.0	4.4	6.8	9.6	12.6	15.8	19.5	23.4	27.5
25	2.1	4.5	7.1	10.0	13.1	16.5	20.3	24.4	28.6
26	2.2	4.7	7.4	10.4	13.6	17.2	21.1	25.3	29.8
27	2.3	4.9	7.7	10.8	14.1	17.8	21.9	26.3	30.9
28	2.4	5.1	8.0	11.2	14.7	18.5	22.7	27.3	32.1
29	2.5	5.3	8.3	11.6	15.2	19.1	23.5	28.3	33.2
30	2.6	5.5	8.6	12.0	15.7	19.8	24.3	29.3	34.4
31	2.7	5.6	8.9	12.4	16.2	20.5	25.2	30.2	35.5

Figure 82. Windage chart for 168-grain .308 Match—Meters—MOA.

168-g Sierra MK; MV 2600 fps; BC .462; Temp 70°F; Elevation 600 ft

Wind Value	Range in Yards									
	100y	200y	300y	400y	500y	600y	700y	800y	900y	1000y
	MOA	MOA	MOA	MOA	MOA	MOA	MOA	MOA	MOA	MOA
1	0.1	0.1	0.2	0.3	0.3	0.4	0.5	0.6	0.7	0.8
2	0.1	0.3	0.4	0.6	3.6	0.8	0.9	1.1	1.3	1.6
3	0.2	0.4	0.6	0.9	0.9	1.2	1.4	1.7	2.0	2.4
4	0.3	0.5	0.8	1.2	1.2	1.5	1.9	2.2	2.6	3.2
5	0.3	0.7	1.1	1.5	1.6	1.9	2.3	2.8	3.3	4.0
6	0.4	0.8	1.3	1.7	1.9	2.3	2.8	3.4	3.9	4.8
7	0.5	1.0	1.5	2.0	2.2	2.7	3.3	3.9	4.6	5.6
8	0.5	1.1	1.7	2.3	2.5	3.1	3.8	4.5	5.2	6.3
9	0.6	1.2	1.9	2.6	2.8	3.5	4.2	5.0	5.9	7.1
10	0.7	1.4	2.1	2.9	3.1	3.9	4.7	5.6	6.6	7.9
11	0.7	1.5	2.3	3.2	3.4	4.3	5.2	6.1	7.2	8.7
12	0.8	1.6	2.5	3.5	3.7	4.7	5.6	6.7	7.9	9.5
13	0.9	1.8	2.7	3.8	4.0	5.0	6.1	7.3	8.5	10.3
14	0.9	1.9	2.9	4.1	4.4	5.4	6.6	7.8	9.2	11.1
15	1.0	2.0	3.2	4.4	4.7	5.8	7.0	8.4	9.8	11.9
16	1.1	2.2	3.4	4.6	5.0	6.2	7.5	8.9	10.5	12.7
17	1.1	2.3	3.6	4.9	5.3	6.6	8.0	9.5	11.1	13.5
18	1.2	2.4	3.8	5.2	5.6	7.0	8.5	10.1	11.8	14.3
19	1.3	2.6	4.0	5.5	5.9	7.4	8.9	10.6	12.4	15.1
20	1.3	2.7	4.2	5.8	6.2	7.7	9.4	11.2	13.1	15.9
21	1.4	2.8	4.4	6.1	6.5	8.1	9.9	11.7	13.8	16.7
22	1.5	3.0	4.6	6.4	6.8	8.5	10.3	12.3	14.4	17.4
23	1.5	3.1	4.8	6.7	7.2	8.9	10.8	12.9	15.1	18.2
24	1.6	3.3	5.0	7.0	7.5	9.3	11.3	13.4	15.7	19.0
25	1.6	3.4	5.3	7.3	7.8	9.7	11.7	14.0	16.4	19.8
26	1.7	3.5	5.5	7.5	8.1	10.1	12.2	14.5	17.0	20.6
27	1.8	3.7	5.7	7.8	8.4	10.5	12.7	15.1	17.7	21.4
28	1.8	3.8	5.9	8.1	8.7	10.8	13.2	15.6	18.3	22.2
29	1.9	3.9	6.1	8.4	9.0	11.2	13.6	16.2	19.0	23.0
30	2.0	4.1	6.3	8.7	9.3	11.6	14.1	16.8	19.7	23.8

Figure 83. Windage chart for 6mm BR—Yards—MOA.

107-g Sierra 6mm BR; MV 2900 fps; Temp 80°F; Elevation 600 ft

Wind Value	Range in Meters								
	100m	200m	300m	400m	500m	600m	700m	800m	900m
	MOA								
1	0.1	0.1	0.2	0.3	0.3	0.4	0.5	0.6	0.7
2	0.1	0.2	0.4	0.5	0.7	0.9	1.0	1.2	1.4
3	0.2	0.4	0.6	0.8	1.0	1.3	1.6	1.8	2.2
4	0.2	0.5	0.8	1.1	1.4	1.7	2.1	2.5	2.9
5	0.3	0.6	1.0	1.3	1.7	2.1	2.6	3.1	3.6
6	0.4	0.7	1.1	1.6	2.1	2.6	3.1	3.7	4.3
7	0.4	0.9	1.3	1.8	2.4	3.0	3.6	4.3	5.0
8	0.5	1.0	1.5	2.1	2.7	3.4	4.1	4.9	5.8
9	0.5	1.1	1.7	2.4	3.1	3.8	4.7	5.5	6.5
10	0.5	1.2	1.9	2.6	3.4	4.3	5.2	6.1	7.2
11	0.7	1.4	2.1	2.9	3.8	4.7	5.7	6.8	7.9
12	0.7	1.5	2.3	3.2	4.1	5.1	6.2	7.4	8.6
13	0.8	1.6	2.5	3.4	4.4	5.5	6.7	8.0	9.4
14	0.8	1.7	2.7	3.7	4.8	6.0	7.2	8.6	10.1
15	0.9	1.9	2.9	4.0	5.1	6.4	7.8	9.2	10.8
16	1.0	2.0	3.1	4.2	5.5	6.8	8.3	9.8	11.5
17	1.0	2.1	3.2	4.5	5.8	7.2	8.8	10.5	12.3
18	1.1	2.2	3.4	4.8	6.2	7.7	9.3	11.1	13.0
19	1.1	2.3	3.6	5.0	6.5	8.1	9.8	11.7	13.7
20	1.2	2.5	3.8	5.3	6.8	8.5	10.3	12.3	14.4
21	1.3	2.6	4.0	5.5	7.2	9.0	10.9	12.9	15.1
22	1.3	2.7	4.2	5.8	7.5	9.4	11.4	13.5	15.9
23	1.4	2.8	4.4	6.1	7.9	9.8	11.9	14.1	16.6
24	1.4	3.0	4.6	6.3	8.2	10.2	12.4	14.8	17.3
25	1.5	3.1	4.8	6.6	8.6	10.7	12.9	15.4	18.0
26	1.6	3.2	5.0	6.9	8.9	11.1	13.4	16.0	18.7
27	1.6	3.3	5.2	7.1	9.2	11.5	14.0	16.6	19.5
28	1.7	3.5	5.3	7.4	9.6	11.9	14.5	17.2	20.2
29	1.7	3.6	5.5	7.7	9.9	12.4	15.0	17.8	20.9
30	1.8	3.7	5.7	7.9	10.3	12.8	15.5	18.4	21.6

Figure 84. Windage chart for 6mm BR—Meters—MOA.

107-g Sierra 6mm BR; MV 2900 fps; Temp 80°F; Elevation 600 ft

Wind Value	Range in Yards									
	100y	200y	300y	400y	500y	600y	700y	800y	900y	1000y
1	0.1	0.1	0.2	0.2	0.3	0.3	0.4	0.5	0.6	0.6
2	0.1	0.2	0.3	0.4	0.5	0.7	0.8	1.0	1.1	1.2
3	0.2	0.3	0.5	0.6	0.8	1.0	1.2	1.4	1.7	1.8
4	0.2	0.4	0.6	0.8	1.1	1.3	1.6	1.9	2.2	2.5
5	0.3	0.5	0.8	1.1	1.4	1.7	2.0	2.4	2.8	3.1
6	0.3	0.6	0.9	1.3	1.6	2.0	2.4	2.9	3.3	3.7
7	0.3	0.7	1.1	1.5	1.9	2.4	2.8	3.3	3.9	4.3
8	0.4	0.8	1.2	1.7	2.2	2.7	3.2	3.8	4.4	4.9
9	0.4	0.9	1.4	1.9	2.5	3.0	3.6	4.3	5.0	5.5
10	0.5	1.0	1.6	2.1	2.7	3.4	4.0	4.8	5.5	6.1
11	0.5	1.1	1.7	2.3	3.0	3.7	4.4	5.2	6.1	6.7
12	0.6	1.2	1.9	2.5	3.3	4.0	4.8	5.7	6.6	7.4
13	0.6	1.3	2.0	2.8	3.5	4.4	5.2	6.2	7.2	8.0
14	0.7	1.4	2.2	3.0	3.8	4.7	5.6	6.7	7.7	8.6
15	0.7	1.5	2.3	3.2	4.1	5.0	6.1	7.1	8.3	9.2
16	0.8	1.6	2.5	3.4	4.4	5.4	6.5	7.6	8.8	9.8
17	0.8	1.7	2.6	3.6	4.6	5.7	6.9	8.1	9.4	10.4
18	0.9	1.8	2.8	3.8	4.9	6.0	7.3	8.6	9.9	11.0
19	0.9	1.9	2.9	4.0	5.2	6.4	7.7	9.0	10.5	11.6
20	1.0	2.0	3.1	4.2	5.4	6.7	8.1	9.5	11.0	12.3
21	1.0	2.1	3.3	4.5	5.7	7.1	8.5	10.0	11.6	12.9
22	1.1	2.2	3.4	4.7	6.0	7.4	8.9	10.5	12.1	13.5
23	1.1	2.3	3.6	4.9	6.3	7.7	9.3	10.9	12.7	14.1
24	1.2	2.4	3.7	5.1	6.5	8.1	9.7	11.4	13.2	14.7
25	1.2	2.5	3.9	5.3	6.8	8.4	10.1	11.9	13.8	15.3
26	1.3	2.6	4.0	5.5	7.1	8.7	10.5	12.4	14.3	15.9
27	1.3	2.7	4.2	5.7	7.4	9.1	10.9	12.8	14.9	16.5
28	1.4	2.8	4.3	5.9	7.6	9.4	11.3	13.3	15.4	17.2
29	1.4	2.9	4.5	6.2	7.9	9.7	11.7	13.8	16.0	17.8
30	1.5	3.0	4.7	6.4	8.2	10.1	12.1	14.3	16.5	18.4

Figure 85. Windage chart for 6.5 Lapua—Yards—MOA.

139-g Lapua 6.5; MV 3200 fps; BC .615; Temp 80°F; Elevation 600 ft

Wind Value	Range in Meters								
	100m	200m	300m	400m	500m	600m	700m	800m	900m
	MOA	MOA	MOA	MOA	MOA	MOA	MOA	MOA	MOA
1	0.1	0.1	0.2	0.2	0.3	0.4	0.4	0.5	0.6
2	0.1	0.2	0.3	0.5	0.6	0.7	0.9	1.0	1.2
3	0.2	0.3	0.5	0.7	0.9	1.1	1.3	1.6	1.8
4	0.2	0.4	0.7	0.9	1.2	1.5	1.8	2.1	2.4
5	0.3	0.6	0.9	1.2	1.5	1.8	2.2	2.6	3.0
6	0.3	0.7	1.0	1.4	1.8	2.2	2.7	3.1	3.6
7	0.4	0.8	1.2	1.6	2.1	2.6	3.1	3.7	4.2
8	0.4	0.9	1.4	1.9	2.4	3.0	3.5	4.2	4.9
9	0.5	1.0	1.5	2.1	2.7	3.3	4.0	4.7	5.5
10	0.5	1.1	1.7	2.3	3.0	3.7	4.4	5.2	6.1
11	0.6	1.2	1.9	2.6	3.3	4.1	4.9	5.7	6.7
12	0.6	1.3	2.0	2.8	3.6	4.4	5.3	6.3	7.3
13	0.7	1.4	2.2	3.0	3.9	4.8	5.8	6.8	7.9
14	0.8	1.6	2.4	3.3	4.2	5.2	6.2	7.3	8.5
15	0.8	1.7	2.6	3.5	4.5	5.5	6.7	7.8	9.1
16	0.9	1.8	2.7	3.7	4.8	5.9	7.1	8.4	9.7
17	0.9	1.9	2.9	4.0	5.1	6.3	7.5	8.9	10.3
18	1.0	2.0	3.1	4.2	5.4	6.7	8.0	9.4	10.9
19	1.0	2.1	3.2	4.4	5.7	7.0	8.4	9.9	11.5
20	1.1	2.2	3.4	4.7	6.0	7.4	8.9	10.5	12.1
21	1.1	2.3	3.6	4.9	6.3	7.8	9.3	11.0	12.7
22	1.2	2.4	3.8	5.1	6.6	8.1	9.8	11.5	13.3
23	1.2	2.6	3.9	5.4	6.9	8.5	10.2	12.0	13.9
24	1.3	2.7	4.1	5.6	7.2	8.9	10.7	12.5	14.6
25	1.4	2.8	4.3	5.8	7.5	9.2	11.1	13.1	15.2
26	1.4	2.9	4.4	6.1	7.8	9.6	11.5	13.6	15.8
27	1.5	3.0	4.6	6.3	8.1	10.0	12.0	14.1	16.4
28	1.5	3.1	4.8	6.5	8.4	10.3	12.4	14.6	17.0
29	1.6	3.2	4.9	6.8	8.7	10.7	12.9	15.2	17.6
30	1.6	3.3	5.1	7.0	9.0	11.1	13.3	15.7	18.2

Figure 86. Windage chart for 6.5 Lapua—Meters—MOA.

139-g Lapua 6.5; MV 3200 fps; BC .615; Temp 80°F; Elevation 600 ft

Wind speed in Kms/hour	Range in meters								
	100	200	300	400	500	600	700	800	900
0	0	0	0.4	0.9	1.8	3	4.6	6.9	9.8
5	0	1.6	4	8	14	22	32	45	59
10	1	3	8	15	26	40	60	83	109
15	1	5	12	22	38	59	87	121	158
20	1	6	15	29	50	78	115	159	208
25	2	8	19	37	62	97	143	197	258
30	2	10	23	44	74	115	170	235	307

Figure 87. Windage chart for 5.56 NATO—Meters—Drift in Inches.

Wind speed in Kms/hour	Range in meters								
	100	200	300	400	500	600	700	800	900
0	0.0	0.0	0.1	0.2	0.3	0.5	0.6	0.8	1.0
5	0.3	0.7	1.2	1.8	2.5	3.3	4.2	5.1	6.0
10	0.6	1.4	2.4	3.4	4.7	6.1	7.8	9.4	11.0
15	1.0	2.3	3.6	5.0	6.9	8.9	11.3	13.8	16.0
20	1.3	2.7	4.5	6.6	9.1	11.8	14.9	18.1	21.0
25	1.6	3.6	5.8	8.4	11.3	14.7	18.6	22.4	26.1
30	2.0	4.5	7.0	10.0	13.5	17.4	22.1	26.7	31.0

Figure 88. Windage chart for 5.56 NATO—Meters—Drift in Minutes.

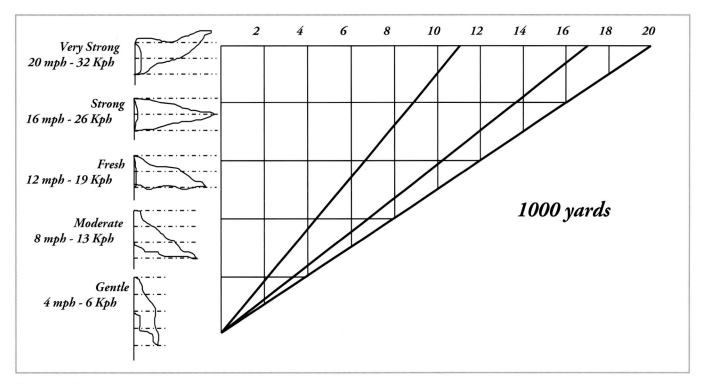

Figure 89. Windage flag diagram—1,000 yards.

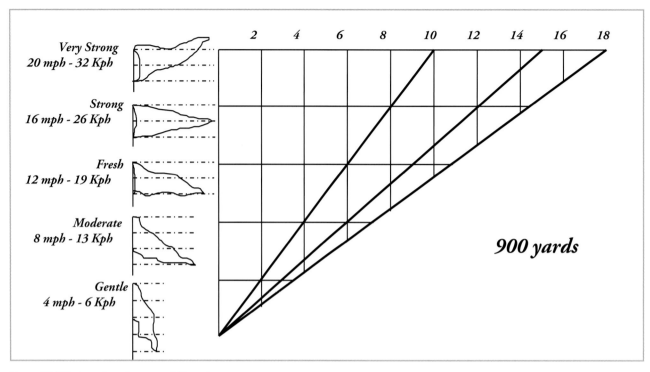

Figure 90. Windage flag diagram—900 yards.

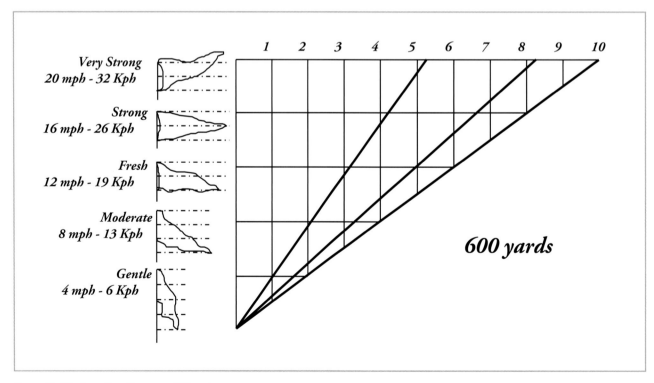

Figure 91. Windage flag diagram—600 yards.

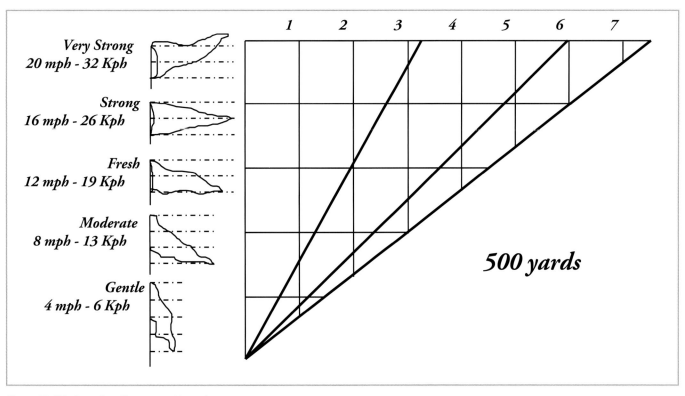

Figure 92. Windage flag diagram—500 yards.

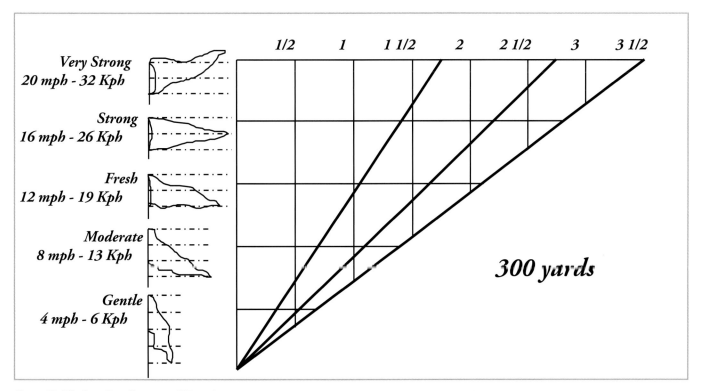

Figure 93. Windage flag diagram—300 yards.

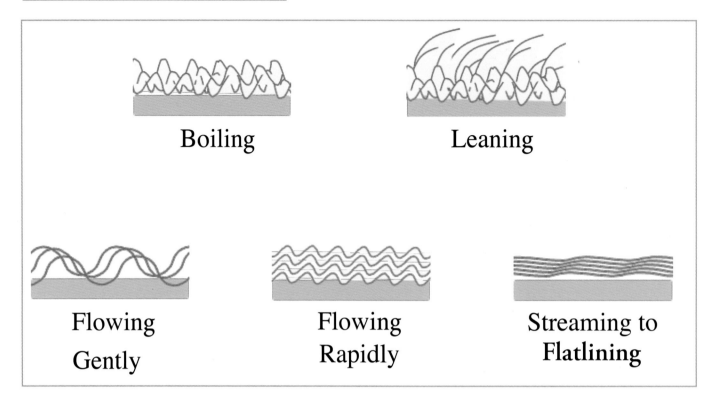

Figure 94. Mirage diagram.

Wind Speeds			
Kph	Mph	Mph	Kph
1	0.6	1	1.6
2	1.2	2	3.2
3	1.9	3	4.8
4	2.5	4	6.4
5	3.1	5	8
6	3.7	6	9.7
7	4.3	7	11.3
8	5	8	12.9
9	5.6	9	14.5
10	6.2	10	16.1
11	6.8	11	17.7
12	7.5	12	19.3
13	8.1	13	20.9
14	8.7	14	22.5
15	9.3	15	24.1
16	9.9	16	25.7
17	10.6	17	27.4
18	11.2	18	29
19	11.8	19	30.6
20	12.4	20	32.2
21	13	21	33.8
22	13.7	22	35.4
23	14.3	23	37
24	14.9	24	38.6
25	15.5	25	40.2
26	16.1	26	41.8
27	16.8	27	43.4
28	17.4	28	45.1
29	18	29	46.7
30	18.6	30	48.3

Range Lengths			
Meters	Yards	Yards	Meters
100	109	100	91
200	219	200	183
300	328	300	274
400	437	400	366
500	547	500	457
600	656	600	549
700	765	700	640
800	874	800	732
900	984	900	823
		1000	914

Figure 95. Metric-English conversion tables.

APPENDIX B: BIBLIOGRAPHY AND OTHER RESOURCES

"Great spirits have always found violent opposition from mediocrities. The latter cannot understand it when a man does not thoughtlessly submit to hereditary prejudices but honestly and courageously uses his intelligence."

—Albert Einstein

ENDNOTES

Introduction

1. Desmond T. Burke, *Canadian Bisley Shooting*, 1970, pp. 133–134.
2. G. David Tubb, *Highpower Rifle*, 1993.
3. "Minutes" refers to the sight setting in minutes of angle. A minute of angle (MOA) is a fraction of a circle (1/21,600). For shooting purposes, it is commonly thought of as being equivalent to 1 inch at 100 yards. That is, a sight change of 1 minute will move your group 1 inch at 100 yards. Because minutes refer to angles, the farther you are from your target, the greater the movement; that is, a sight change of 1 minute will move your group 5 inches at 500 yards and 10 inches at 1,000 yards. Most sights are calibrated in minutes, with smaller increments in ¼ minutes. Some shooters refer to the smaller increments on their sights as "clicks" (because the mechanism gives a small "click" as the sight is adjusted) whether they are ¼ minutes or some other measure.

Chapter 1

1. Bill McRae, *Outwitting the Wind* (publication unknown).
2. External ballistics is the science of the bullet in flight.
3. A fairly average kind of handload has the 155-grain bullet traveling at 2,900 fps (muzzle velocity). This roughly translates to a speed of 1,977 mph. All shooters strive to ensure that their bullet speed does not drop below the speed of sound before it passes through the target; the speed of sound is roughly 818 mph. The average of these is about 1,397 mph.
4. Thanks to Clint Dahlstom for pointing this out and Jim Bullock for confirming it.
5. FBI Academy Firearms Training Unit, *Advanced Rifle Training;* see www.firearmstactical.com/pdf/fbi_observer_sniper_manual.pdf.
6. Norm Barber, a well-known Canadian F-Class shooter and a meteorologist by trade, explains it this way: The reason humid air is less dense than dry air is due to the atomic weights of the molecules making up dry or humid air. Dry air is around 75 percent N_2 (atomic weight 28) and 25 percent O_2 (atomic weight 32). In humid air, some of the 28- and 32-weight molecules are displaced by H_2O molecules (atomic weight 18). Thus the more H_2O in the air, the more 18-weight molecules are displacing the heavier 28- and 32-weight molecules and the given volume is less dense, or lighter.
7. Charles F. Young, "Wind Reading—Another Way of Looking at It?" *Tactical Shooter* (April, 1998).

8. Our friend Wordsworth Price advises that, in purely scientific terms, "velocity" has both magnitude and direction, while "speed" is the correct term to refer to magnitude only. Therefore, strictly speaking, one should not talk about velocity and direction, but rather speed and direction. However, as Wordy observed, it is likely that everyone knows what we mean.

9. Desmond T. Burke, *Canadian Bisley Shooting: An Art and a Science*, 1970, p. 123.

10. In fact, at most ranges, the flags are considerably above the line of flight of the bullet. As Clint Dahlstrom stated in his notes to us following the publication of the first edition of *The Wind Book*: "Flags are almost always a lot higher than the culminating level of bullet path, which is about 10 feet. The 'standard' 1,000-yard flag is 15 feet long and 6 feet wide at the halyard, which means that with zero wind, the flag hangs 18 feet from top of pole to the tip of the flag (15 feet plus half of the 6-foot width). The usual clearance of the flag tip above the ground is about 6 feet or so, which indicates that the middle of the flag is about 21 feet above the ground."

11. E.G.B. Reynolds and Robin Fulton, *Target Rifle Shooting*, 1972.

12. Burke, *Canadian Bisley Shooting*, p. 123

13. As we will discuss later, wind from the left moves the bullet to the right and requires left windage to correct; in short, left wind requires left windage on the sight.

14. A headwind increases bullet drag (air resistance), and this affects the velocity and the trajectory, resulting in a slight difference in vertical displacement (completely negligible at less than 600 yards, and only about two-thirds of a minute of angle at 1,000 yards). Since wind rarely shifts from a pure headwind to a pure crosswind during a shoot, this effect is usually not an issue; the shooter usually builds the vertical deflection into his elevation requirement on the day.

15. Whereas decimal targets are typically scored X, 10, 9, 8, 7, etc., Bisley-style targets are typically scored V (V-bull), 5 (bull's-eye), 4 (inner), 3 (magpie), 2 (outer), although there are some local variations.

16. Mirage can also be seen in cold climates, just not as reliably. It can often appear over snow on a bright winter's day, but it can be flighty and hard to read. The appearance of mirage depends on layers of air at various temperatures, and moisture in the air makes the mirage more visible.

17. In doing research for this book, we have found that there is definitely room for controversy here. Surveyors using optical methods assure us that they will work at night to minimize the effect of heat waves distorting their readings. Benchrest shooters swear they can see that the image of the target has moved with their well-mounted rifles and powerful scopes. For practical purposes, any change in elevation would be consumed in the day's sight setting, except for the circumstance where the intermittent clouds produce intermittent mirage. Under this circumstance, the shooter may well need to make elevation adjustments to accommodate the mirage.

18. Young, "Wind Reading—Another Way of Looking at It?"

19. More efficient calibers will usually fly flatter and faster, but the principles of understanding their time in flight are the same.

20. For the reader who is interested in the mathematical formulas, the clearest and most thorough explanation that we have found is in Burke's *Canadian Bisley Shooting*.

21. While 700 yards in not shown on this chart, the deflection is approximately 11¾ minutes of angle for a wind at 20 mph.

22. Burke, *Canadian Bisley Shooting*, p. 117.

23. While the bullet is moving more slowly for the second half of its flight, under most circumstances this decrease in velocity has only a slight effect on deflection. To prove this to yourself, run your ballistics software with bullets traveling different velocities. In practical terms, there are factors far greater in wind reading than the small differences caused by decelerating bullets.

24. As you will read in the "What Others Say" section following, the difference required is extreme.

25. One of the students in our Wind-Reading Course was MWO David Atkins, a member of an artillery unit in the Canadian Forces. He commented that it was very clear that a near-muzzle ricochet would have far greater deflection than a near-target deflection. The same goes for wind deflection.

26. Burke, *Canadian Bisley Shooting*, p. 131.

27. For diagrams of these three examples, see John Simpson's "Words of Wisdom" in chapter 5.

28. To make correct adjustments you must also know your sight. Target rifle sights are usually in genuine minutes and quarter minutes, although they come in British/US or Australian minutes (which are different-sized measures). Telescopic sights are often built with either quarter-minute or third-minute clicks, and then scaled with four clicks to the "minute," so that the size of the minute can be coarser or finer. Smallbore sights are usually adjusted in terms of "clicks" and rotations, and at least one expert in smallbore shooting says that top smallbore shooters lose more points by not knowing their sights than in not judging the wind correctly.

29. The Plot-o-Matic (EZ-Graf) is an ingenious device used to assist the shooter in keeping the group centered and interpreting wind conditions. It is further described and discussed in chapter 3 in the section on recording methods and tools.

Chapter 2

1. George Stidworthy, "Reading the Wind," *Rifle* magazine (March/April 1981).

2. For more information about developing a game plan, see chapter 3, "Techniques and Tactics."

3. For details on using flags, bookends, and primary and secondary conditions, see chapter 3, "Techniques and Tactics."

4. G. David Tubb, *Highpower Rifle*, 1993.

5. Charles F. Young, "Wind Reading—Another Way of Looking at It?" *Tactical Shooter* (April, 1998).

6. Ibid.

7. The Plot-o-Matic (EZ-Graf) is an ingenious plotting device described in chapter 3.

8. Young, "Wind Reading—Another Way of Looking at It?".

9. Burke, *Canadian Bisley Shooting*, p. 133.

10. Ibid, p. 131.

11. E.G.B. Reynolds and Robin Fulton, *Target Rifle Shooting*, 1972.

12. Young, "Wind Reading—Another Way of Looking at It?".

13. Burke, *Canadian Bisley Shooting*, p. 128.

Chapter 3

1. Linda K. Miller, "Snatch the Pebble," *Precision Shooting* (July 2000), and *Favorite Stories on Winning*, 2003.

2. Desmond T. Burke, *Canadian Bisley Shooting*, 1970, p. 123.

3. We have observed elite shooters in hard wind conditions use their "angle flag" as the primary indicator. They find their mean sight setting for that angle, and then they tune their actual sight setting with an assessment of the wind velocity.

4. Burke, *Canadian Bisley Shooting*, p. 123.

5. The basic math is in *Canadian Bisley Shooting*, and considerable details are shown in two *Tactical Shooter* articles: "Kentucky Windage Goes High-Tech" and "The Question Is Blowin' in the Wind."

6. Snowbound winter evenings are a typically Canadian thing! Readers from other countries need to substitute the local conditions that would keep them from being out at the range.

7. Burke, *Canadian Bisley Shooting*, p. 123.

8. These devices are commonly available in stores that cater to recreational sailors and yachtsmen. We have tried several and have found that the ones with the exposed wind vanes are a little too fragile, and we prefer the ones that have shrouded wind vanes.

9. The availability of ballistics software is improving rapidly. A recent Internet search yielded several promising packages, most of which offered a 30-day free trial.

10. The wind flag diagrams are built from data for 7.62 NATO-issue ammunition. The observant reader will notice that the windage chart in Figure 45 shows that the 155-grain Sierra bullet with a muzzle velocity of 3,100 fps requires considerably less windage correction.

11. Bill Richards made these remarks when he spoke to the Ontario Team to Bisley at the Millennium Matches in the

year 2000. The Ontario Team graciously included us at this team function. Bill's "words of wisdom" are also included in chapter 5 of this book.

12.   George Chase's words of wisdom are also included in this book.

13.   George Chase showed us a neat trick. He draws a little pictogram of the wind flag (angle and/or velocity) that goes with each group right above the group, so he can quickly see what sight setting he needs.

14.   The "theory of a group" establishes that when a series of shots are fired from a rifle at the same point of aim, they will seldom pass through the same hole. Instead they create a pattern on the target called a group. It also provides that the size of the group will increase in proportion to the range.

15.   Target rifle shooters use .308 ammunition, iron sights, and a sling, all of which increase their group size, compared to F-Class shooters, who use any caliber, telescopic sights, and a bipod or front rest.

16.   This is entirely different from (but would certainly add to the effect of) "Burke's bulges," which are group deformities caused by canting errors, as described in *Canadian Bisley Shooting*, pp. 96–109.

17.   Miller, "Snatch the Pebble" *Precision Shooting* (July 2000) and *Favorite Stories on Winning*.

18.   Burke, *Canadian Bisley Shooting*, p. 134.

19.   "Recce" is a British term, short for reconnaissance.

20.   Charles F. Young, "Wind Reading—Another Way of Looking at It?" *Tactical Shooter*, (April 1998).

21.   Burke, *Canadian Bisley Shooting*, p. 131.

22.   We have used this exercise in some of our courses, where we emphasize that because the reading you will get is dependent on the angle you read from, it is essential that you align your spotting scope with your line of fire.

23.   That would be a 49 out of a 50 possible score, a fine long-range score in good conditions and an outstanding one on a blustery day! From *Canadian Bisley Shooting*, p. 125.

24.   Burke, *Canadian Bisley Shooting*, p. 120.

25.   Data taken from the Parker wind calculator.

26.   These data are taken from commonly available plotting diagrams—notice small differences from the Parker

chart information in the previous figure. If you run ballistics software for your own .308 load, you will find further small differences.

27.   Burke, *Canadian Bisley Shooting*.

28.   When we teach our wind-reading course, we use the team setup to separate the roles of firing the perfect shot (the shooter), centering the group (the plotter), and reading the wind (the wind coach). We do this so that each person can focus on one job at a time, and so build the skills required to do each job well. While acting as wind coach, the student can watch the wind all the time, including when the shot is being fired. Most students are surprised by how much the wind can change during those last few seconds.

29.   Young, "Wind Reading—Another Way of Looking at It."

30.   Burke, *Canadian Bisley Shooting*, p. 133.

31.   G. David Tubb, *Highpower Rifle*, 1993.

32.   Burke, *Canadian Bisley Shooting*, p. 124

Chapter 4

1.   Linda K. Miller and Keith A. Cunningham, "How Good Shooters Think," *Favorite Stories on Attitude*, 2003.

2.   Desmond T. Burke, *Canadian Bisley Shooting*, 1970.

3.   E.G.B. Reynolds and Robin Fulton, *Target Rifle Shooting*, 1972.

4.   Raymond Von Wahlde, "Kentucky Windage Goes High-Tech: Development of a Laser Crosswind Sensor," *Tactical Shooter* (March 1999).

5.   Charles F. Young, "Wind Reading—Another Way of Looking At It?" *Tactical Shooter* (April 1998).

6.   Burke, *Canadian Bisley Shooting*, p. 125.

Chapter 5

1.   One mile is 5,280 feet or 1760 yards or 1609 meters.

2.   "Burke's bulges" refers to the group that results from canting errors; Desmond T. Burke, *Canadian Bisley Shooting*, 1970, pp. 96–109.

3.   This reminds us of the old Canadian saying: "If we are attacked by a bear in the bush, I don't have to outrun the bear—I only have to outrun you!"

4. Added to the second edition of *The Wind Book.*

5. Added to the second edition of *The Wind Book.*

6. *The Canadian Marksman* is the journal of the Dominion of Canada Rifle Association.

7. The values are representative of issue ammunition, originally very likely IVI. Your own rifle/ammunition combination may well require slightly different base numbers. For example, the numbers yielded for 500 yards in these charts is almost exactly Linda's .308 rifle/ammo requirement for 600 yards.

BIBILOGRAPHY

BOOKS

Burke, Desmond T. *Canadian Bisley Shooting: An Art and a Science.* 1970.

Department of the Army. *Sniper Training and Employment.* Training Circular No. 23–14, Washington, D.C., June 14, 1989.

Karas, Lester W. *Competitive Shooting Excellence with the High Power Target Rifle.* 1975.

Miller, Linda K. and Keith A. Cunningham. *Favorite Stories on Attitude.* MilCun Marksmanship Complex, 2003.

_____. *Favorite Stories on Winning.* MilCun Marksmanship Complex, 2003.

Owens, M.Sgt. James R. *Reading the Wind and Coaching Techniques.* Milwaukee, WI: JAFEICA Publishing, 1996.

Patrick, Special Agent Urey W. *Advanced Rifle Training for the Observer/Sniper.* Firearms Training Unit, FBI Academy, Quantico, Virginia. (www.firearmstactical.com/pdf/fbi_observer_sniper _manual.pdf)

Reynolds, E.G.B. and Robin Fulton. *Target Rifle Shooting.* London: Barrie & Jenkins Ltd., 1972.

Sweet, James. *Competitive Rifle Shooting,* 6th Edition. (Shooting Book Publisher, P.O. Box 355, Maroubra, NSW, Australia) 1973.

Tubb, G. David. *Highpower Rifle.* Clifton, CO: Zediker Publishing.

PERIODICALS

McKellar, C.A. "On the Range, Calculated Success." *Hunting & Shooting,* January/February 1997.

McRae, Bill. "Outwitting the Wind." (Publication unknown.)

Miller, Linda K. "Snatch the Pebble." *Precision Shooting,* July 2000.

Pocock, Ed III. "All You Need to Know About Wind, Part I." *Tactical Shooter,* June 2000.

Simpson, John C. "The Question Is Blowin' in the Wind." *Tactical Shooter,* August 2000.

Stidworthy, George. "Reading the Wind." *Rifle,* March/April, 1981.

Von Wahlde, Raymond. "Kentucky Windage Goes High-Tech: Development of a Laser Crosswind Sensor." *Tactical Shooter,* March 1999.

Young, Charles F. "Wind Reading—Another Way of Looking at It?" *Tactical Shooter,* April 1998.

OTHER RESOURCES

Plot-o-Matic, Plot-o-Matic Owner's Manual, and Plot-o-Matic Accessory Pack (redesigned under the name EZ-Graf): available through MilCun Marksmanship Complex at www.milcun.com

Wind meters and weather stations: a search on the Internet will yield a good variety of these devices.

ABOUT THE AUTHORS

Linda K. Miller has more than 25 years of business experience, including business planning, management, marketing, and information systems. She has considerable experience in international smallbore target shooting as a member of Canada's Shooting Team. She has won medals at the 1993 Mexico World Cup, the 1994 Commonwealth Games, and the 1995 Cuba World Cup. In 1999, Linda became the first woman to win the Ontario Lieutenant Governor's Medal for fullbore shooting; these competitions have a proud and honored history of over 150 years. In 2002, Linda shot F-Class and became the top female provincially, nationally, and at the world championships. Linda is also an accomplished and internationally certified marksmanship coach. She is the editor of *CoachNet,* a periodical for coaches, a designer of courses for competitive and professional marksmen, and an author of numerous articles on shooting skills.

Capt. Keith A. Cunningham (Ret.) is a career military officer with more than 25 years' experience with the Canadian Forces and the US Army. He has considerable practical experience, including a combat tour in Vietnam, peacekeeping and countersniper operations in Cyprus, and annual unit- and command-level military exercises in North America and Europe. Keith has taught marksmanship courses at the Canadian Forces Infantry School and at several police forces in Ontario. Keith is an internationally certified shooting coach and has successfully coached numerous teams to national and international excellence. Keith is also an internationally renowned gunsmith with more than 25 years' experience, specializing in long-range practical rifles. He has built and regulated rifles for competitors around the world. Keith is a prize-winning international rifle and pistol competitor, having won honors at Bisley, at the World Long Range Championships, and at the Commonwealth Games. He is a member of the Canadian Forces Sports Hall of Fame and all three of the Dominion of Canada Rifle Association Halls of Fame.

Keith and Linda hold many provincial and national titles and records, including being the only couple to have both won the Ontario Provincial Championship (Keith in 1990, 1995, 2003, and 2004; Linda in 1999). They are also one of the few couples who have been members of Canadian national fullbore teams, having been members of the PALMA team competing in South Africa in 1999, and of the team shooting at the Millennium Target Rifle World Championships at Bisley in 2000. They are popular guest lecturers and speakers, and their articles on marksmanship have been published in shooting magazines such as *Precision Shooting, The Accurate Rifle, Tactical Shooter, The Canadian Marksman, The Canadian Forces Infantry Journal,* and *Aim* magazine.

ABOUT MILCUN MARKSMANSHIP COMPLEX

The purpose of our business is to promote competitive marksmanship and to educate and train both recreational and professional marksmen. MilCun Marksmanship Complex is a registered Ontario company, founded in 1996. It offers the following services:

- Gunsmithing—complete line of gunsmithing services, specializing in long-range rifles for the competitive marksman as well as the police sniper; we offer a line of custom-made rifles for competitive and professional use.
- Marksmanship training—competitive marksmanship courses, including technical and mental skills; we also offer a complete line of police sniper courses.

- Consulting—we provide consulting services to coaches, trainers, program developers, range developers, and marksmanship businesses of all types.
- Range facilities—we operate a range facility in Haliburton County, Ontario, Canada, approximately two hours from metropolitan Toronto. This includes a 100-meter range, a 600-meter conventional range, a 1,000-meter range, a field firing range, and a classroom.

Keith is the chief operations officer, chief instructor, and head gunsmith. Linda is the chief executive officer and coaching specialist. You can contact Keith or Linda through MilCun at www.milcun.com.